ISAAC BASHEVIS SINGER

A Study of the Short Fiction

Also available in Twayne's Studies in Short Fiction Series

Twayne's Studies in Short Fiction

Gordon Weaver, General Editor
Oklahoma State University

ISAAC BASHEVIS SINGER
Drawing by Rebecca Frieda Alexander

ISAAC
BASHEVIS
SINGER

A Study of the Short Fiction

Edward Alexander
University of Washington

TWAYNE PUBLISHERS • BOSTON
A Division of G. K. Hall & Co.

Twayne's Studies in Short Fiction Series No. 18

Copyright 1990 by G. K. Hall & Co.
All rights reserved.
Published by Twayne Publishers
A division of G. K. Hall & Co.
70 Lincoln Street
Boston, Massachusetts 02111

Copyediting supervised by Barbara Sutton.
Book design and production by Janet Z. Reynolds.
Typeset in Caslon 540 by Crane Typesetting Service, West Barnstable,
Massachusetts.

First published 1990.
10 9 8 7 6 5 4 3 2 1

Library of Congress Cataloging-in-Publication Data

Alexander, Edward, 1936–
    Isaac Bashevis Singer : a study of the short fiction / Edward
Alexander.
        p.   cm. — (Twayne's studies in short fiction : no. 18)
    Includes bibliographical references and index.
    ISBN 0-8057-8329-6 (alk. paper)
    1. Singer, Isaac Bashevis, 1904–   —Criticism and interpretation.
2. Singer, Isaac Bashevis, 1904–   —Interviews.   3. Authors,
Yiddish—United States—Interviews.   I. Title.   II. Series.
PJ5129.S49Z575   1990
839'.0933—dc20
                                                                    90-37724
                                                                        CIP

TO MY GRANDPARENTS
OF BLESSED MEMORY

Fanny and Morris Alexander
Fannie and Louis Levy

Contents

Contents

Preface

> They hated him for the amazing thing that had happened to
> him—his fame—but this they never referred to. Instead they
> discussed his style: his Yiddish was impure, his sentences
> lacked grace and sweep, his paragraph transitions were amateur,
> vile. Or else they raged against his subject-matter, which was
> insanely sexual, pornographic, paranoid, freakish—men who
> embraced men, women who caressed women, sodomists of
> every variety, boys copulating with hens, butchers who drank
> blood for strength behind the knife. All the stories were set in
> an imaginary Polish village, Zwrdl, and by now there was almost
> no American literary intellectual alive who had not learned to
> say Zwrdl when he meant lewd.
>
> —*Cynthia Ozick, "Envy; or, Yiddish in America"*

Irving Howe has often remarked upon the paradox whereby the very
modernism that arouses suspicion and resentment among Yiddish readers of Singer's fiction has been the basis of his extraordinary and (for
a Yiddish writer) unparalleled popularity among literary intellectuals
whose ignorance of Yiddish is equaled by their indifference to such
parochial Jewish concerns as national survival. Howe points out that
many intelligent and experienced Yiddish writers are uneasy, even
impatient and angry, with Singer's work because of his "heavy stress
upon sexuality . . . , concern for the irrational, expressionist distortions
of character," and his indifference to the Yiddishist traditions of sentimentality and social justice. Among devotees of literary modernism,
however, "for whom the determination not to be shocked has become
a point of honor,"[1] these same characteristics have contributed as much
to his high reputation as the less accidental traits of stylistic brilliance
and narrative invention.

The modernism that has brought such differing reactions from the
Yiddish and the non-Yiddish reading audiences is contained mainly in
Singer's voluminous output of short stories. The novels operate within

the old-fashioned traditions of nineteenth-century realism and deal, unmistakably, with questions of the national destiny of the Jewish people. Although it may not be correct to read the short stories as modernist excursions into diabolism, perversity, and apocalypse, entirely cut off from Singer's novelistic concerns with Jewish religion and Jewish destiny, we can hardly doubt that this is how they are generally read. Whatever may be the reasons for Singer's popularity as a short story writer with the readers of the *New Yorker*, *Playboy*, and *Esquire*, it is safe to assume that a passionate interest in things Jewish and in the tragic course of Jewish history is not among them. The hordes of students who flock to hear Singer at places like Charlottesville, Virginia, or Madison, Wisconsin, may reasonably be supposed to have a keener interest in dybbuks and spooks than in the destroyed Jewish world of Eastern Europe. There may even be a dark political significance in the fact that some of the most ecstatic praise of Singer's modernist brilliance as a short story writer has appeared in such journals as the *New York Review of Books*, which nobody ever accused of being unduly concerned with the well-being of Jews.

Nevertheless, the wide appeal of Singer's stories among readers ignorant of, and indifferent to, Jewish religion, history, and peoplehood is of literary importance because it disproves the fashionable literary prejudice that holds that writing about Jews is an insuperable obstacle to universal appeal. Many critics who have blithely assumed that it is the natural destiny of the human race, or of that part of it which reads books, to puzzle over Blake's Zoas, Yeats's gyres, and Pound's socioeconomic ravings are brought up short at the prospect of reading books about Jews because, they maintain, the concerns of Jews are not those of universal humanity. Anyone familiar with the body of criticism about the writings of Saul Bellow (not excluding some of that writer's unhappy utterances about his own work) will know that it is one of the smelly little orthodoxies of American literary criticism that the Jewish writer (and he alone) is compelled to choose between writing about the experience of his people and addressing himself to the principle of Mankind and therefore to humanity as a whole.

Singer writes almost always as a Jew, to Jews, for Jews; and yet he is heard by everybody. The audience of Yiddishists often resents him for some of the reasons that it resented Sholem Asch: getting translated, reaching the great non-Jewish public through translation, and then writing for translation. But not even this resentful and suspicious body of readers can accuse Singer of doing as Asch seemed to them to do, writing explicitly Christian stories in order to gain a wide audience.

Singer's tremendous success among critics as well as ordinary readers seems to illustrate the truth of Cynthia Ozick's contention that, contrary to the apostles of universalism, great literature never consciously seeks to be "universal": "Dante made literature out of an urban vernacular, Shakespeare spoke to a small island people, Tolstoy brooded on upper-class Russians. Yeats was the kindling for a Dublin-confined renascence. They did not intend to address the principle of Mankind; each was, if you will allow the infamous word, tribal. Literature does not spring from the urge to Esperanto, but from the tribe."[2] Singer understood, as did Allen Tate of Tennessee, William Faulkner of Mississippi, and Flannery O'Connor of Georgia, that a writer needs what Singer calls an address, for a real artist is rooted in his milieu, in his people, in his environment. Singer himself has always recognized that it was only by examining, and not by avoiding, his own memories and experiences as a Jew that he could penetrate to the memories and experiences of mankind, which is an infinitely varied repetition. He once stated in an interview that "we Jews have been living in an eternal, permanent crisis. Life itself is a permanent crisis, but the Jews really live in a more permanent crisis."[3]

My critical approach to Singer is, I hope, one that would win the approval of the author himself. Here a personal anecdote may be revealing. Singer once told me of the splendid hospitality he had received from a famous American literary critic at whose university Singer had lectured. But he also insinuated a sly criticism of the man, who had been among the first American importers of the designer philosophies of contemporary European literary critical theory: "Just before I boarded the plane he gave me a copy of the first issue of his new journal of literary theory. I tried to read it on the plane, but unfortunately I couldn't understand a word of it. Of course, I'm only a writer."

Like Singer, I have tried to address myself to what Dr. Johnson in his life of Thomas Gray called "the common reader: for by the common sense of readers, uncorrupted by literary prejudices, after all the refinements of subtlety and the dogmatism of learning, must finally be decided all claims to literary honors." I take this statement to mean that the critic must recognize that his task is to assist the reader who comes to literature with the expectation that it will add something to his moral awareness and humane understanding. If so, then, as Allen

Tate used to say, "critical style ought to be as plain as the nose on one's face."

For typing parts of the manuscript I am grateful to Dorothy Becker, Dee Carroll, and Marianna Wright; for compiling the index, I thank Anne Berkbigler.

Edward Alexander

University of Washington

Notes

1. Introduction to *Selected Short Stories of Isaac Bashevis Singer* (New York: Modern Library, 1966), xvi, xii.
2. "America: Toward Yavneh," *Judaism* 19 (Summer 1970): 275.
3. Morton A. Reichek, "Storyteller," *New York Times Magazine*, 23 March 1975, 28.

Acknowledgments

I am grateful to the following publishers and journals for permission to use previously published material.

"An Interview with Isaac Bashevis Singer" by Joel Blocker and Richard Elman. *Commentary* 37 (November 1963). Reprinted by permission of the American Jewish Committee. "Singer's Paradoxical Progress" by Ruth Wisse. *Commentary* 67 (February 1979). Reprinted by permission of the American Jewish Committee.

"The Fame of Bashevis Singer" by Jacob Glatstein. *Congress Bi-Weekly*, 27 December 1969. Reprinted by permission of the American Jewish Congress.

Conversations with Isaac Bashevis Singer by I. B. Singer and Richard Burgin. New York: Doubleday, 1985. Reprinted by permission of Doubleday.

"The Shtetl World" by Irving Feldman. First published in the *Kenyon Review* 24, no. 1 (Winter 1962). © 1962 by Kenyon College. Reprinted by permission.

"Yiddish Tradition vs. Jewish Tradition: A Dialogue" by I. B. Singer and Irving Howe. *Midstream* 19 (June/July 1973). Reprinted by permission of *Midstream*.

"Isaac Bashevis Singer: Conversations in California" by David M. Andersen. *Modern Fiction Studies* 16 (Winter 1970–71). © 1970 by Purdue Research Foundation, West Lafayette, Indiana. Reprinted by permission.

Excerpts from Irving Howe's introduction to *Selected Short Stories of Isaac Bashevis Singer*, edited, with an introduction, by Irving Howe. New York: Random House, 1966. © 1966 by Random House, Inc. Reprinted by permission of Random House, Inc.

Excerpts from *Isaac Bashevis Singer on Literature and Life: An Interview with Paul Rosenblatt and Gene Koppel*. Tucson: University of Arizona Press, 1979. Reprinted by permission of the publisher.

"Envy; or, Yiddish in America" by Cynthia Ozick, *The Pagan Rabbi and Other Stories*. New York: Alfred A. Knopf, 1971. © 1969 by Cynthia Ozick. Reprinted by permission of Random House, Inc.

Part 1

THE SHORT FICTION

Introduction

The following discussion of Singer's short fiction comprises nine sections. These sections are not logically parallel to one another, for some stress Singer's imaginative modes, others his characteristic topics and favorite themes. I begin with a survey of autobiographical stories that reveal Singer's attitude toward his craft and toward the ingrained expectation of the audience of Yiddish readers that their writers should fulfill many of the national and communal functions that were fulfilled for other peoples by the nation-state (something Jews did not have until the establishment of Israel in 1948). Three of Singer's characteristic imaginative modes are next discussed. The supernatural tales show how his mistrust of the reality of material phenomena expresses itself in an openness to the supernatural and demonic elements of experience. The section on his moral tales explores Singer's habits of ethical interpretation and his attempt to extract the moral essence of a form of religious faith he no longer shares. His use of archetypes is then analyzed as the imaginative expression of a powerful Jewish sense of memory combined with a weak Jewish sense of history, the fictional reflection of a sense of the past that is circular rather than linear.

Somewhere in the border country between a mode and a favorite theme is the group of Singer stories of apocalypse. These tales usually express his guilty fascination with the messianic impulse in Jewish life and his disapproval of the modern form of that impulse: political utopianism.

Perhaps the richest, most abundant vein of Singer's genial powers is his fiction about the relations between man and God and the conflict between faith and doubt. Few modern writers have so fully committed themselves to a belief in belief itself and to a contempt for incredulity as a form of gullibility commonly called worldliness. The only other theme to which Singer has returned as obsessively is that of the relations between the sexes, a subject he has called inexhaustible. His "marriage group" is as varied as that of Chaucer's *Canterbury Tales*, but he has

3

also ventured imaginatively into the manifold perversions to which love is liable. The penultimate section of my discussion deals with Singer's "vegetarian" tales. He has called vegetarianism his only dogma and has tenaciously clung to the view that as long as people apply the principle of "might makes right" in their dealings with animals, they must not be surprised if the Almighty deals likewise with them.

Finally, some of the stories that treat (nearly always indirectly) the Holocaust—the destruction of European Jewry by National Socialism —are examined as expressions of the desire of Singer, as a writer of fiction, to dream into existence a vanished world.

Readers of this book should be aware that it considers Singer as what he has often said he is: a writer in the Jewish tradition but not exactly the Yiddish tradition. Although there is something suspect and disingenuous in Singer's eagerness to distance himself from his Yiddish predecessors, and I have often pointed to similarities between his stories and theirs, it is nevertheless true that he exists for a large part of his readership in what Cynthia Ozick has called New Yiddish. By this she means a Jewish dialect of English in the sense that "old" Yiddish was a Jewish dialect of Middle High German. Singer has eased the creation of this literary hybrid by working closely with his translators: indeed, he does most of the translation into English from the point of view of Yiddish. As a result, these "translators" are in most cases more like collaborators or editors. Singer takes the work of translation with utmost seriousness, and has said that to him the translation becomes as dear as the original. But it should be remembered that scores of Singer's short stories have never been translated into English. The stories examined in this book are those by which Singer has chosen to make himself known to the English reader, those which have earned him his international reputation and the Nobel Prize in literature. I have omitted discussion of works never translated, and therefore little known beyond a small and (outside the academy) rapidly diminishing audience—albeit an audience that makes up in quality of response what it lacks in quantity. I have also left out of consideration Singer's stories for children, despite their distinction and great popularity.

Autobiographical Stories:
Portraits of the Artist

Increasingly during his later years, Singer has written stories that are thinly veiled segments of autobiography. In the three early collections of stories translated into English, this genre does not appear. In the fourth volume, *The Séance*,[1] we have one story, "The Lecture," that is distinctly in Singer's autobiographical voice. In the fifth collection, *A Friend of Kafka*,[2] a number of obviously autobiographical tales appear, among them "Guests on a Winter Night," "Dr. Beeber," "The Mentor," "Schloimele," and "The Son," a story that touches on the painful subject of Singer's meeting, after a separation of twenty years, with the son he had by his first love. By the time of *A Crown of Feathers*[3] (1973), autobiographical tales predominate.

Singer's blurring of the distinction between fiction and fact, imagination and history, has been the subject of a shrewd study of his narrative strategies—David Neal Miller's *Fear of Fiction*.[4] Without entering, as Miller does, into the theoretical questions that arise from this blending, we may recognize that Singer has written numerous stories that are autobiographical, even where they contradict, in matters of details, the facts of his own life.

In some of these stories the imaginative pressure is very low and the distinction between fiction and memoir nearly invisible. In others— and these are not only the more interesting but also the ones that tell us more about their author—the narrator places himself midway between the real Isaac Bashevis Singer and a number of imagined voices and personae that dramatize the conflicting impulses of Singer's inner world or draw out into extreme form principles and ideas we know to have been held by the author himself. A convenient way of suggesting the range of the autobiographical stories is to glance at some of the many tales dealing with Singer's career as a Yiddish writer and, therefore, with the fate of Yiddish itself in the aftermath of the Holocaust.

Singer's ambivalence about his role as a Yiddish writer and about his relation to the Jewish cultural heritage, as well as to the various political

5

projections of the Jewish future, derives from his ambivalence about the Enlightenment. A cursory glance at the stories, still more the novels, that deal with the *haskalah*, or Jewish Enlightenment, would suggest that Singer is an avowed enemy of its antitraditionalism, its zeal to emulate the gentiles, and its tendency toward moral laxity, especially sexual promiscuity. Nevertheless, we must remember—as Singer himself surely does—that without the Enlightenment the very conception of a secular Jewish literary tradition would not have arisen. The orthodox religious tradition that Singer the novelist often defends against the heterodoxies of Enlightenment rationalism and antinomianism had spoken very clearly to the young Singer against his chosen career. In an interview, Singer once said: "They [the religious] considered all the secular writers to be heretics, all unbelievers—they really were too, most of them. To become a *literat* was to them almost as bad as becoming a *meshumed*, one who forsakes the faith. My father used to say that secular writers like Peretz were leading the Jews to heresy. He said everything they wrote was against God. Even though Peretz wrote in a religious vein, my father called his writing 'sweetened poison,' but poison nevertheless."[5]

Singer's accounts of his youth, whether fictional or "factual," indicate how irresistible was this Enlightenment "poison" to him. In "Guests on a Winter Night" (in *A Friend of Kafka*), he provides a vivid portrait of his older brother Israel Joshua, who preceded him on the path to worldliness and enlightenment. In his shortened coat, hair, and memory, his progressive rhetoric, his espousal of the "advancing" west against the retrograde "Asiatics," Israel Joshua is the prototype of dozens of his brother's fictional characters:

> Joshua wore a long gaberdine and a small cap. He had sidelocks, too, but they were trimmed. Joshua had become enlightened—"spoiled," my father called it. He refused to study the Talmud, he read secular books, he was opposed to the use of a matchmaker. . . . Joshua insisted that Jews in Poland lived like Asiatics. He mocked their sidelocks, their gaberdines down to their shoe tops. How much longer were they going to study the law concerning the egg that was hatched on a holiday? Europe, my brother said, had awakened, but the Jews of Poland were still in the Middle Ages. (26–27)

Isaac listened to the endless disputes between his brother and father, and was always on the "enlightened" side of the argument. His father's promises that when the Messiah came those who studied the Torah would be saved and the unbelievers would perish were not convincing to the young man.

The story of Isaac Bashevis Singer's enlightenment continues in a tale entitled "Three Encounters" (in *Passions*).[6] Here the young man who tells the story leaves home at age seventeen because he has lost faith in the Gemara and the Shulchan Aruch and does not wish to become a rabbi or to have his marriage arranged by a matchmaker. After three years in Warsaw, where his brother tries to help him, he is forced to return home, "with congested lungs, a chronic cough, no formal education, no profession, and no way that I could see of supporting myself in the city" (268). His father, recently appointed rabbi of Old-Stikov in Eastern Galicia, warns him to curb his heretical impulses for the family's sake, but salvation from the constrictions of provincial life comes in the form of his brother's offer of the job of proofreader of a Warsaw literary weekly the brother is now coediting.

Before the narrator returns to Warsaw, however, he meets a beautiful girl named Rivkele who has been engaged, without her consent, to her father's apprentice. No sooner does the narrator—whom we may confidently call Singer—hear this news than he tries to undermine the girl's faith in the old religious ways, in the Jewish community, and in her engagement. Although he claims that he was already disenchanted with the Enlightenment, he felt perversely that he had a kind of duty to preach all its clichés to her: "The people lived in filth, knew nothing about hygiene, science, or art. This was no town—I spoke dramatically —but a graveyard" (252). Offering himself as the apotheosis of *haskalah*, he "cried like a seducer in a trashy novel," exhorting Rivkele to "escape from this mudhole." Yet even as he urges her to flee—with him—he has "the odd feeling that this wasn't I talking but the dybbuk of some old enlightened propagandist speaking through my mouth" (274). In a peculiar twist of irony, it is not religion but Enlightenment that practices a double standard, preaching to fools according to their folly, inculcating "progressive" beliefs that have already failed those who preach them.

"Three Encounters" passes severe judgment upon the "enlightened" writer who espouses an iconoclasm he no longer believes in. Nine years later, when Rivkele seeks out Singer in New York, it is to report that she has gone still further down the path on which he started her, having converted to Roman Catholicism in a disastrous marriage to a criminal. Now, however, she wants to repent, to "be a Jewish

7

daughter again," but to do so through the man who—so she insists once again—was responsible for her degradation. But the once-ambivalent enlightener refuses: although he has accepted responsibility in the abstract, he will not try to undo the terrible consequences of his words of eleven years earlier. Singer has sometimes been commended for his untrustworthiness in relation to Jewish traditional or even merely national culture, his refusal to be a cultural "spokesman." But here the author presents the darker side of this authorial autonomy; the narrator's unreliability, from the Jewish point of view, has ruinous consequences for the human being upon whom he tries out, as if she were the object of a literary experiment, Enlightenment ideas.

Although Singer does mischief in "Three Encounters" through the spoken rather than the written word, the moral danger inherent in his more "enlightened" fiction is the burden of several stories. A good example is "The Third One" (*A Crown of Feathers*), in which a reader tells Singer how the undoing of his marriage is connected "actually with your writing—not with you personally" (213). Zelig Fingerbein recounts how he and his formerly modest wife became sexually imaginative, "progressive," and promiscuous by imitating "the situations from your stories in the Yiddish papers." His wife, Genia, aspired to emulate the nymphomaniac tendencies of certain women in Singer's novels, such as Hadassa (*The Family Moskat*)[7] and Clara (*The Manor*).[8] Singer, the man if not the writer, seems dismayed by his reader's tale of the dissolution of his marriage, and is promptly scolded for not facing up to the predictable consequences of his stories: "Why are you so shocked? You write like a modern man, but here you are with the old morals and prejudices" (220). The possibility remains that Fingerbein is a poor interpreter of Singer's fiction—the author reserves judgment on his critic in this story—and it is a commonplace that works of literature are radically defenseless against the uses and misuses to which they are put. Yet the frequency with which Singer depicts the baneful effects of the Enlightenment strain in his fiction, a strain that appears to outlive the writer's conscious repudiation of it, suggests an uneasiness about secular writing that might well remind us of his father's troglodyte suspicion that even the best of it is "sweetened poison."

It is the justified boast of Yiddish literature that it was based on a peculiarly intimate relationship between authors and readers for whom storytelling was a communal activity. The greatest Yiddish writers addressed a living, responding audience, not cultivated members of the middle class, and certainly not literary coteries. When I. L. Peretz died in 1915, seventy-five thousand people came to his funeral in Warsaw, and Sholem Aleichem's funeral the following year was attended by a similar number in New York; such demonstrations of popular affection were unmatched with respect to any other writers of modern literature. Singer has never achieved the status of the classical Yiddish masters within the community of Yiddish readers, and is even looked upon with some degree of reserve and suspicion by them. Yet many of Singer's stories turn on the mixture of attractions and dangers in being a writer whose audience values and exploits the fact that it lives, so to speak, next door to him. "The Admirer" (*Passions*) might stand as a prototype of the many stories in which the writer is sucked into the lives of his readers, most of whom recognize no distinction between the author and the man, much less the narrator and the author.

In "The Admirer" a writer who is clearly Singer himself is visited by an admirer who says she has replaced her husband with Singer's books, which have become the essence of her being. Although the narrator gripes about the frequency with which his correspondents and visitors turn out to be "eccentrics—odd, lost souls"—it is clear that Singer relishes this form of flattery. Then it turns out that the books aren't enough, at least not for Singer's female readers: "Since I've started reading you, you've become the lover in my fantasies—you have driven off all the others" (63). Singer's impassioned admirer is half-deranged, and while in his apartment has, or pretends to have, an epileptic seizure. Within two hours of her arrival, all hell has broken loose in the author's life, he curses the day he was born, and he fears he will not survive this visit. The story thus becomes an ironic comment on the dangers (as well as the satisfactions) of appealing to a living, responding audience.

In another story, called "The Yearning Heifer" (*Passions*), the writer tries to escape from his profession and his admirers by going off to the Catskill Mountains, only to find that the man who leaves town takes not only himself but also his admirers with him. Even in the provinces the readers of his newspaper column are on the watch for him and, if female, ready to throw themselves at him. (There is something unseemly in the frequency with which Singer shows women smitten by his literary aura, an impression not entirely offset by the occasional stories, such as "The New Year Party" [Passions], in which readers consult him as an authority on abstruse religious questions.)

"The New Year Party" is one of several stories that afford Singer the opportunity to reiterate his refusal to subordinate his art to politics.

"Leftist writers," the narrator complains, "scolded me for failing to promote world revolution. The Zionists reproached me for not dramatizing the struggle of the Jewish state and the heroism of its pioneers" (163). Singer's gloomy view of politics in general and utopianism in particular is everywhere evident in his stories. In "The Magazine" (*A Crown of Feathers*) we are told how the writers of Germany and Russia had prostituted themselves to, respectively, Hitler and Stalin. In addition, "the writers from Poland jumped on the Communist bandwagon. They became Bolsheviks overnight—the Labor Zionists, the Bundists, the Folkists, and the Independents" (174). In reply to Zeinvel Gardiner, who doggedly clings, through forty years of failure, to his belief that the world can be saved by writers (in little magazines) who will "awaken" the just, Singer says that the just will always sleep. "They can be woken up," insists Gardiner. "If they're woken up," replies Singer, "they'll become wicked" (175). Thus, paradoxically, the writer who abjures what activists call his political responsibility does more good even in the political realm than those who foolishly rouse sleeping monsters from the deep.

But a far more compelling theme for Singer than the question of the writer's relation to his audience has been the question of whether, in the aftermath of the breakup of eastern European Jewish culture and of the Holocaust, it is even possible to continue writing in Yiddish. Stories such as "A Day in Coney Island" suggest that Singer was beset by such fears when he first came to America. In this obviously autobiographical tale, collected in *A Crown of Feathers*, Singer tells of a thirty-year-old Yiddish writer from Poland who fears that, because he has only a tourist visa, he will be deported to the land of his birth and there fall victim to Hitler. Although the editor of a Yiddish paper has published a few of the writer's stories, the editor has also complained that no one in America "gave a hoot about demons, dybbuks, and imps of two hundred years ago." The writer-narrator was, he recalls, himself afflicted by doubts and by the fear that at age thirty he was already an anachronism: " 'Who needs Yiddish in America?' I asked myself" (31).

Just how profound was the young Singer's uneasiness about the future of Yiddish writing in America may be seen in an essay entitled "Problems of Yiddish Prose in America," published in 1943, eight years after his arrival in the United States. In the essay Singer alleges that the better Yiddish prose writers avoid writing about American Jewish life because they cannot convey in Yiddish the speech and thought of young American Jews, and have long since exhausted whatever interest lay in the elderly immigrants: "Words, like people, sometimes endure a severe disorientation when they emigrate, and often they remain forever helpless and not quite themselves. This is precisely what happened to Yiddish in America." The Yiddish writer who tries to nourish himself on contemporary American Jewish life is likened by Singer to a man dining on leftovers: "only food prepared in the old world can nourish him in the new." In 1943 Singer was convinced that Yiddish literature could never transcend its ghetto origins and address the world as an equal. Its hope lay not in the future, but in the past. "When turned towards 'universal' ends," he argues, "Yiddish becomes a caricature of a language. However, it is filled with untapped potential to reveal our past and create art works thematically bound to that past. . . . When she [Yiddish] starts talking about the past . . . pearls drop from her lips. She remembers what happened fifty years ago better and more clearly than what happened this morning."⁹

The paradoxical mixture of gloom and hope expressed in this essay, published just after Singer had ended his (alleged) seven years' silence as a writer of fiction, is also reflected in "A Day in Coney Island." Although the story's narrator practices ironic self-depreciation—referring frequently to the irrelevance of a writer who dwells, and in Yiddish, on werewolves, sprites, and other themes "no one cares about and nobody believes in" (41)—our knowledge that the narrator is none other than Singer himself, who has gained a worldwide reputation, fame and fortune, and a Nobel Prize for writing about such irrelevant frivolities, does much to offset this impression of hopelessness.

There is another kind of autobiographical tale in which Singer explores the ambiguous relationship between the modern Yiddish writer and the experience of modern Jewry. If "A Day in Coney Island" exemplifies Singer's realistic approach to this subject, and "The Lecture" (discussed elsewhere in this book) his surrealistic one, "The Last Demon" (*Short Friday*)¹⁰ might tentatively be called his supernatural one. Of the many stories in which Singer uses a first-person narrator who bears marked resemblances to the author, none comes so close as this one does to representing his inner relationship to his own work. The narrator tells of his plight as the last remaining demon, whose occupation is gone because man himself has become a demon: to proselytize for evil in these times would be carrying coals to Newcastle. Like Singer himself, the last demon has been deprived of his subject, the Jews of Eastern Europe. "I've seen it all," he says, "the destruction of Tishevitz, the destruction of Poland. There are no more Jews, no more demons. . . . The community was slaughtered, the holy books burned, the cemetery desecrated." Like Singer, the last demon attempts to speak as if history had *not* destroyed his subject and as if he could defy time: "I speak in the present tense as for me time stands still" (120). Like Singer, finally, the demon must sustain himself on dust and ashes and Yiddish books: "I found a Yiddish storybook between two broken barrels in the house which once belonged to Velvel the Barrelmaker. I sit there, the last of the demons. I eat dust. . . . The style of the book is . . . Sabbath pudding cooked in pig's fat: blasphemy rolled in piety. The moral of the book is: neither judge, nor judgment. But nevertheless the letters are Jewish. . . . I suck on the letters and feed myself. . . . Yes, as long as a single volume remains, I have something to sustain me" (130).

By a cruel historical paradox, Yiddish, once the language of everyday uses, the *mameloshen*, or mother tongue, subservient to the holy tongue of Hebrew, has, because of its now-permanent association with the martyrdom of Eastern European Jewry, become a holy tongue (while Hebrew often seems, in Singer's eyes at least, to have become in Israel a language used for the most mundane purposes, not excluding the purchase of "pig's fat" in Tel Aviv by people he often views as Hebrew-speaking gentiles). The remnants of this holy tongue can now be discovered only by the most diligent of its devotees.

The motif of Yiddish texts hidden away in old barrels appears once again in "The Colony" (*A Friend of Kafka*), a bitter tale about the writer's visit to the Jewish colony in Argentina. The patio of the hostel where he stays has a billiard table and barrels filled with torn books. Looking into one of the barrels, he finds the standard Yiddish library of his youth: Sholem Aleichem, I. L. Peretz, and Lamed Shapiro, plus the usual Yiddish translations of European classics. But the new generation of Argentinian Jews has given up Yiddish for Spanish. If its members occasionally bring in a Yiddish writer or actor, they do so mainly to avoid criticism from the Yiddish press in Buenos Aires. "There still remained two or three old people who might enjoy these activities" (207). The visiting writer delivers a speech about Jewish history and Yiddish literature, but "the boorish men and fat women in the audience seemed not to understand what I said. . . . There was something Biblical in that abandoning of one's origins, forgetting the efforts of the fathers. To this spiteful generation there should have come a prophet, not a writer of my kind." When somebody asks him why he is rummaging among the books in the barrel, he says, "I am visiting my own grave."

The Yiddish books in the barrels of "The Last Demon" and "The Colony" are waiting for a Yiddish redemption. But Singer knows that, whatever his great gifts may be, he cannot assume the role of national/ cultural spokesman or prophet. Given the tremendous, unprecedented popularity and critical acclaim Singer has gained, it may seem that his career belies these elegies over Yiddish which themselves, after all, belie the lament over the inability to continue writing in a dead language about a dead—a murdered—civilization. And yet these stories are elegies, for Singer remains aware not merely of his own limitations, but also of the impossibility of resurrecting, even in literature, a destroyed civilization.

Supernatural and
Demonic Tales

In one of his interviews, Singer offered at least three different reasons for his use of the demonic and supernatural in his stories. The first was economy: "By using Satan or a demon as a symbol, one can compress a great many things. It's a kind of spiritual stenography." The second reason was symbolism: "Instead of saying this is the way things happen, I will say, this is the way demons behave. Devils symbolize the world for me, and by that I mean human beings and human behavior." But Singer hastened to add that his devils were more than literary instruments, since he really believed in their substantial existence. His third reason for using them, therefore, was that in fact *they* used *him*: "Every serious writer is possessed by certain ideas or symbols, and I am possessed by my demons" (Blocker/Elman, 371). His demons are powerful symbols in Singer's work because they are realities first.

Singer's openness to the supernatural realm and his consequent desire to wrench readers out of their limiting naturalist complacencies are evident in a story like "Jachid and Jechidah" (*Short Friday*). The ruling idea of this tale is the Wordsworthian conceit (as in the "Immortality" ode) that we die into life, trailing clouds of glory from our divine home. A female angel named Jechidah has, for the sin of blaspheming against and denying God, been sentenced to death, that is, "descent to that cemetery called Earth" (82). In Sheol—a halfway house en route to death, which human beings mistakenly call life—Jechidah already feels keenly the loss of such heavenly pleasures as the music of the spheres, the perfumes of paradise, meditation on the secrets of the Torah, and (this above all) the companionship of her lover, Jachid. As much as she regrets what has been lost, she fears the unknown future, about which she has heard terrifying rumors: "A dead soul immediately began to rot and was soon covered with a slimy stuff called semen. Then a grave digger put it into a womb" (82). The more religious, God-fearing angels claim that death in the earthly prison is only a temporary torture and that the soul will ultimately be liberated from the horrors of flesh,

14

blood, marrow, and nerves. But Jechidah, "being a modernist" (83), is shut out from the comforts and consolation of belief in resurrection of the soul.

Dying into earthly life, Jechidah grew up in the normal way, in a family of other dead souls, and attended the institutions of learning— high schools and universities—that are charged with preparing "corpses" for the countless mortuary functions to be performed in a huge necropolis. Inured to earthly habits, she (like all the souls whom she symbolizes) mistakes death for life, and yearns to follow the instinct of female corpses and use her womb as "a grave for the newly dead" (86).

By happy coincidence, she falls in love with Jachid, her soul mate from their prior existence, their true home. Neither recognizes the other, yet Jechidah has the feeling that they have experienced all this before, "in some other world" (88). Jachid, on the other hand, is a medical student whose mind has been constricted by the materialistic monism of positivist scientific education: he "knows" that earth is the only world. If his logic is followed, thinks Jechidah, "if there is no soul and life is nothing but a short episode in an eternity of death, then why shouldn't one enjoy oneself without restraint?" (89). By implication, then, belief in immortality of the soul is essential to human morality.

It is only in sleep and dreams that human beings, "the dead," glimpse the home from which they have been exiled, and therefore the possibility of returning to it from the transient illusion, the trial and testing, which is death on earth. This glimpse is sufficient to enable Jechidah to recognize that all of creation, including copulation, is part of God's plan. Her imminent insemination by Jachid is the burial of yet another dead soul, but, if viewed under the aspect of eternity, it is imbued with a larger meaning, an intimation of immortality absent from the naturalistic dogma that no life exists before or after life on earth.

"Jachid and Jechidah" supplies the metaphysical foundation for Singer's rejection of worldliness as a form of gullibility. It suggests the tenuousness of our accepted standards and valuations, and the strong possibility that what we hold to be the goods of the world are really its evils, and its ultimate calamity, death, truly a release, a return to the only true life.

That Singer has no consistent theory of the supernatural will at once be evident from the slight tale called "The Warehouse" (*The Séance*), which recounts the conversations of a number of "naked souls" who are waiting, in the lowest heaven, to be reincarnated in new bodies. The warehouse is a bureaucratic chaos, largely the result of contriving useless tasks to keep unemployed angels busy. The chaos explains why human beings so often appear to be ill-composed jumbles of mismatched parts. One impatient soul asks why God doesn't straighten things out, and precipitates a debate between the atheistic souls who deny God altogether and the supervisor, Bagdial, who says the real problem is that God has removed himself to an infinite distance in the seventh heaven and never intervened lower down. But the main point of this jocular, unfocused tale is that the defectiveness of so many human bodies ought to (but does not) disabuse mortals of their dogmatic belief that "the body is everything" (132), a dogma that makes them forget—since "the most defective of all the organs is the portion of the brain containing the memory" (133)—that this "vale of tears" (127) is a temporary exile from the heavenly home.

The essential abnormality, indeed freakishness, of human creatures is a main motif of "Shiddah and Kuziba" (*The Spinoza of Market Street*),[11] one of Singer's most fully imagined, if also enigmatic, supernatural stories. Here, once again, man is viewed under the aspect of eternity; but this time the viewers are devils, not angels, inhabitants of the lower depths, not the celestial heights—and "the lot of man is to creep on the skin of the earth like a louse." As they sit in darkness, nine yards inside the earth, Shiddah explains to her son Kuziba that "man is the mistake of God" (90), the product of a momentary inattention to His beloved Lilith, mother of the demons. As if to mock the Enlightenment idea that God's perfection could be seen in the consummate mechanical design of His human creature, Singer allows his articulate demon to express revulsion at the utterly irrational grotesqueness of the human animal and his grossly imperfect adaptation to nature: " 'Man!' Shiddah spat. 'He has a white skin but inside he is red. He shouts as if he were strong, but really he is weak and shaky. Throw a stone and he breaks. . . . In heat he melts. In cold he freezes. There is a bellows in his chest which has to contract and expand constantly. . . . He stuffs himself with mildew of a kind which grows in mud or sand' " (90–91). Man's chief occupation, according to Shiddah, is doing evil. His chief intellectual characteristic—no surprise in creatures whose "ideas come from a slimy matter which they carry in a bony skull on their necks" (91)—is the arrogance of ignorance: "Some of them even deny our existence. They think life can only breed on the surface of the earth"

(91). Singer's devils, like his angels, always stand ready to justify their author in extending the empire of his imagination from the old world of Europe and the new world of America to the next world, both its upper and lower regions.

This underworld is the realm of darkness and silence. In Singer's symbolic geography, darkness—despite its association with underworld devils—has powerful, often positive connotations that show just how great was the distance he had traveled from Enlightenment assumptions. Singer understands that virtue, like any other plant, will not grow unless its root is hidden. Silence too suggests a profundity beyond the grasp of speech and consciousness. That is why Kuziba's father, Hurmiz, is off at a yeshiva, located thousands of yards deeper in the earth, where he studies the secret of silence, its many degrees, and its culmination in God, who dwells in darkness and silence, not light and noise.

But it is precisely light and noise, conveyed from the human world via "a monstrous, spiraling machine" that comes crashing through the nine yards of rock, crushing and grinding everything "with a cruelty beyond good and evil" (94), that makes an end of their underworld home. Shiddah and Kuziba watch in horror as the miners, who look even more terrifying, filthy, and fierce than the rest of their species, invade the underworld, bringing their dreaded light. Mother and son, cut off from further descent, must perforce climb to the surface. One secondary parabolic drift of the story might suggest that industrial expansion liberates the devils from their lair and enables them to thrive on earth. But the story's primary meaning is that human life is actually enriched by these carriers of darkness, these exiles from the nether-world. Shiddah and Kuzibah accept their fate, seeking temporary con-solation in stories they have heard about man's inability, despite his monstrous greed, to light up every mystery with his intellect and to destroy every forest and desert with his machines. But their ultimate consolation lies in the conviction that "the last victory would be to darkness . . . , a time would come when the light of the Universe would be extinguished . . . , all voices silenced; all surfaces, cut off. God and Satan would be one. The remembrance of man and his abom-inations would be nothing but a bad dream which God had spun out for a while to distract Himself in His eternal night" (95–6).

Although "Jachid and Jechidah," "The Warehouse," and "Shiddah and Kuziba" are told in the third person by a reliable, detached narrator, they are all told from the point of view of the supernatural figures, rather than of the inhabitants of the earth to which they are exiled. In other tales, however, Singer shifts his point of view to this world and keeps simultaneously before the reader two opposed explanations of bizarre events: the natural or psychological one and the demonic alternative. Is "The Black Wedding" (*The Spinoza of Market Street*), we ask, a story of mystical paranoia, or of demonic interference in human affairs? Hindele, the bride in question, descends from a Hasidic dynasty that has practiced cabala, created golems, exorcized dybbuks, and been constantly plagued, in matters small and large, by "vengeful devils." Her father, on his deathbed, advised her to "keep silent if you are to be spared" (28).

Hindele inherits her family's susceptibility to being victimized by mysterious agents. She does not see her husband, Reb Simon, until their wedding, when he lifts her veil. "The moment Hindele saw him she knew what she had suspected long before—that her bridegroom was a demon, and that the wedding was nothing but black magic, a satanic host" (30). Although her physical eye places Hindele in a well-lighted living room, her conviction that her husband is an evil spirit brings a vision of enclosure in a dark forest. Everything appears to her under a double aspect: the young men's sashes are snakes; their Yiddish songs are the hissings of vipers; the bridesmaids are snouted pigs; the groom's relatives are lions, bears, and boars. "Alas, this was not a human wedding, but a Black Wedding. Hindele knew, from reading holy books, that demons sometimes married human virgins whom they later carried away behind the black mountains" (31).

Since her wedding night is spent with a devil, it entails violent rape, in consequence of which Hindele becomes pregnant—a little devil grows inside her, half-frog, half-ape, pushing and tearing at her sides. Once again, however, what seems to Hindele a devilish affliction can be given a perfectly ordinary, naturalistic interpretation. The little devil within her has capricious urges: to eat lime from the wall, the shell of an egg, all kinds of garbage. But might this not be one way of viewing the notorious vagaries of the pregnant woman's appetite? Are the assaults made by a host of devils flaying her and pulling the nipples of her breasts with pliers metaphors for the unspeakable agonies of a woman in labor, or are they literally a supernatural attack? Whatever the case, Hindele's suffering becomes so intense that she can no longer forbear from screaming. As soon as she does so, the threatened fate ensues: she is swallowed in darkness and becomes an unwilling recruit to "the castle of Asmodeus where Lilith, Namah, Machlath, Hurmizah rule" (35). As far as her neighbors know, however, she has "only" died in childbirth.

Singer's imaginative reach beyond the limits of naturalistic, dogmatic common sense may derive from the kind of experience he often recounts in autobiographical tales that contain no supernatural characters but are permeated by a kind of natural supernaturalism. Like many writers before him—Wordsworth, Carlyle, and Newman come to mind—Singer seems at times to doubt the reality of the material world. In a story called "Alone" (*Short Friday*), for example, Singer tells of an experience in Miami Beach that taught him the danger of getting one's wishes fulfilled. Wishing he were alone in a hotel, he soon finds himself the sole guest in a dilapidated dwelling presided over by a hunchbacked Cuban woman. The material world of "Alone" is by no means fleeting or evanescent, but tangible and powerful, making its presence felt in the form of a hurricane. Nevertheless the narrator, alone with himself and his thoughts, is assaulted by questions like "Who is behind the world of appearance? Is it Substance with its Infinite Attributes? . . . Is it the Absolute, Blind Will, the Unconscious? Some kind of superior being has to be hidden in back of all these illusions" (51). The narrator feels "like a ghost, cut off from everything" (52), and wonders whether life may be a dream, his fellow human beings in fact fellow angels or (like the Cuban woman) demons who are deceiving him by putting on the semblance of material existence. This mistrust of the reality of material phenomena, deeply and frequently felt by Singer, underlies the rich imagination of his supernatural tales.

Moral Tales

At the conclusion of a story called "The Gravedigger" (*Passions*), Singer's Aunt Yentel (one of his numerous elderly female narrators) asks the young boy:

> "Do you like stories?"
> "Yes, Aunt, very much."
> "What is the good of stories? You better go and study the Ethics
> of the Fathers."
> "Later." (242–43)

Although Aunt Yentel appears to deprecate the moral value of mere stories compared with that of the pithy apothegms of the Mishnaic treatise compiled by Rabbi Judah the Prince, the exchange may be interpreted very differently. The "good" of stories is of the same kind as, and thus a secular substitute for, rabbinic wisdom; they too may act as a *magister vitae* and guide to ethical behavior.

Singer has, to be sure, often announced (with feigned modesty) that "literature will never replace religion" and that his stories are not created with the rationalistic purpose of "saying" something.[12] On the other hand, he has frequently recalled that he was "brought up in the categories of good and evil. Almost nothing was neutral. Either you did a *mitzvah* or you did an *averah* (sin)" (Burgin, 6). A great many of his stories suggest that here, as in so many other respects, the assumptions of a religious way of life he had apparently rejected remained a more imperious presence in Singer's imaginative life than the brittle doctrines of new, nonreligious faiths he (temporarily) adopted.

Singer was also aware of the extent to which, in a secular society that follows upon the decay of religion, people bereft of the old certainties and traditional authorities might come to view the writer as a sage, a *vates*. Several of his stories describe how Jews resort to him for advice of a kind they would once have sought from rabbis. In "The New Year Party" (*Passions*), for example, a man wants to reveal the depth of his devotion to a dead friend by engraving on the friend's tombstone the (grotesquely inappropriate) inscription "Be healthy and happy wherever you are" (178). The engraver balks at this, but agrees that he will do as requested if the great Isaac Bashevis Singer is consulted and gives his approval, which—after invoking the appropriate quotation from the Talmud—he does.

Some of Singer's moral tales celebrate a particular quality of character. This is clearly the case with the ill-named tripartite story called "Passions" (*Passions*), which offers three illustrations or exempla of the stubborn power of human persistence.

In the first instance, Singer draws on what Maurice Samuel called the ingenious charade that governed the religious and secular life of the Jews of eastern Europe and preserved their folk identity: the pretense that they were still living in their ancient homeland.[13] A simple village peddler named Leib Belkes decides to express his devotion to the Land of Israel by rebuilding the Temple—in a scale model, constructed from fifty packs of matches, exactly according to the specifications of the Talmud. When resentful neighbors, envious of his achievement, destroy his temple—thereby displaying the same causeless hatred that led to destruction of the original temple—he withdraws from life into melancholy and the reading of Yiddish stories about the Land of Israel. He disappears mysteriously, and five years pass before he returns with the stunning news that he has gone, on foot, to the Holy Land, a trek of two years. The story's moral is simple, unambiguous, unshaded by irony: "When a man persists he can do things which one might think can never be done" (296).

The second instance of admirable stubbornness is a pious but ignorant tailor named Jonathan. Like the women, he reads the Bible only in Yiddish, not Hebrew. Shamed publicly in the synagogue on Simchat Torah (Festival of Rejoicing over the Law) by a usurer named Reb Zekele, who has resented Jonathan's being (accidentally) called before himself to carry a Torah scroll, Jonathan vows that in a year he will be a greater scholar than his wealthy and learned antagonist. If he fails, he will sew, for free, a coat made of fox fur for Reb Zekele's wife. Using the hundred guldens he has saved as a dowry for his daughter, Jonathan engages an instructor in Talmud to teach him seven pages of the Talmud each day so that after a year, all thirty-seven tractates will have been mastered: a task of leviathan proportions. But Jonathan studies eighteen hours a day and goes without sleep several nights a week until he has become not merely proficient but a virtual Talmudic wizard and master of Jewish learning in general, one who crushes his opponent when they grapple with each other on the appointed day just before the next Simchat Torah. The triumph of Jonathan's persistence is peculiarly Jewish not only in being an affirmation of the central Jewish value of Torah learning but in vindicating the community of simple men, toilers like himself who have long chafed under the arrogance of the wealthy: "The town seethed like a kettle. Synagogue Street was full of tailors, shoemakers, combers of pig bristles, coachmen, and such. It was their victory" (307). The virtuous Jonathan receives a new house from Zekele—for that was his side of the bet—but gives it to the community to serve as an inn for yeshiva boys and poor travelers. More important, he feels no need to use the knowlege he has acquired as a stepping-stone to higher positions and selves—like rabbi or ritual slaughterer—but appreciates learning's intrinsic value, and returns to the tailor's scissors and iron. The tale thus teaches three lessons: the power of persistence to overcome social disadvantage; the extent to which genius is not so much a natural endowment as an achievement of the will; and the undesirability of making out of Torah learning a "spade for digging," a means to attain something consequent upon itself.

The third and final story in "Passions," supposedly intended to celebrate the creative resources of obsession, does not really belong with the first two, though it is the only one of the three that is adequately described by the title. Rabbi Mendel is a wayward Hasid. Whereas the Hasidim stressed joy and deplored asceticism in all its forms, Rabbi Mendel has "indulged" in fasting, carrying it to such an extreme that he eventually adopts a regimen of fasting from one Sabbath to the next. He also mortifies the flesh by bathing himself in icy water. Finally he makes of his life a perpetual Yom Kippur (Day of Atonement). In doing so, he becomes the object of a slyly insinuated irony. He too, like his Hasidic forebears, is dedicated to joy, but what for others who have strong passions may be self-control is for him a kind of self-indulgence: " 'Those who run after the pleasures of the world,' he tells his followers, 'don't know what pleasure is. For them gluttony, drinking, lechery, and money are pleasures. There is no greater delight than the service of Yom Kippur. . . . The prayers are a joy. There is a saying that from confessing one's sins one does not get fat. It's completely false' " (310). There is also a saying—though Singer tactfully avoids it—that if you don't know how to eat, it is no virtue to fast. The stated moral of the tale—stated, however, by one Meyer Eunuch and not Singer—is that "everything can become a passion, even serving God" (312). The implied moral is far more ambiguous because it raises relativist questions about pleasure and pain and about the ease with which serving oneself can be mistaken for serving God. (The story may have been influenced by, and can be profitably compared with, Israel Joshua Singer's "Repentance," a tale that alleges a certain ruthlessness in the Hasidic devotion to joy, even on Yom Kippur.)

The subject of passions is viewed from another perspective in "The Primper" (*A Friend of Kafka*). As so often is the case in Singer's moral tales, the moral is stated even before its exemplary illustration is given: "A preacher came to our town and he said that everything can become—how do you call it—a passion, even eating sunflower seeds" (182). Adele, at forty, is still a spinster, irredeemably so, because of her ruling passion, a madness for clothes; a linked, secondary passion for cleanliness that leads her to wash constantly while complaining that "all men stink" (182); and an all-consuming vanity that makes her unwilling to bare a birthmark on her breast (191). She is always going for fittings, waiting for the latest fashion magazines from Paris, and dressing up like a bride for the simplest occasions. The husband of the narrator speaks with more prescience than he can imagine when he asks about Adele—by now in her fifties—"For whom is she adorning herself, for the Angel of Death?" (184). The narrator herself, a lifelong friend of Adele, recalls that even in her sixties the "primper" could think and talk of nothing but dresses, jewelry, and the way she and other women decked themselves out—which fact, however, did not prevent her from invariably looking "disheveled and haggard, as if she were sleeping in her garments" (186).

Sleeping in her garments, it turns out, is exactly what Adele has in mind: eternally sleeping. Sensing that she has reached an age when the grave beckons, she makes shrouds for herself out of the most precious linen and silk, hoping to prolong her passion into the world to come. But now her obsession comes into conflict with some of Judaism's most sacred ordinances. Jews are not permitted luxurious burial clothes, for all must be buried alike in plain linen. Having all her life valued her vanity above men, she now prefers it to God as well, at least to the God of Abraham, Isaac, and Jacob. Rather than go to the grave in shameful rags, she converts to Christianity, which offers (to her way of thinking) a mortuary fashion show: "A Christian hearse is decorated with wreaths and the attendants following carry lanterns and are dressed ceremoniously like knights of old. . . . Woe to me, she had equipped herself with a whole trousseau" (190–91). In the event, however, her aspirations are frustrated, for she is buried after a long period of rain, "and her grave was full of water and mud" (191).

The passion held up to scorn and derision in "The Primper" is so different from the perseverance celebrated in "Passions" that Singer could be exonerated from the charge of thematic inconsistency if his narrator did not positively invite it in her generalizing conclusion: "I often say, one cannot become too much taken with anything, not even the Torah" (191). In a curious coda that leads the reader far from the tale just concluded, we hear of "a young scholar who studied Maimonides so much, he became an unbeliever" (191). If we ask, How does this explicit moral lesson square with the unstinting praise for the tailor Jonathan's immersion in the Torah? we shall have to answer, Not too well. But since the implicit lesson of the stories in praise of persistence does not contradict that of the story excoriating uncontrollable obsession, we may say that it is not Singer's aesthetic integrity but his sense of moral discrimination that is open to question.

Singer's moral tales are dominated by the view that, as Irving Feldman[14] has written, there are no gaps in the cosmic order, no places where the power of God and the moral order give way to their Manichaean opposites. The pervasiveness of moral order, its perfect economy, is for Singer especially evident in the fate of language. In "Three Encounters" (*Passions*) he writes: "The lessons of the moral primers came back to me. No word goes astray. Evil words lead to iniquitous deeds. Utterings of slander, mockery, and profanity turn into demons, hobgoblins, imps. They stand as accusers before God" (278).

The almost magical potency of words—especially to inflict mischief even greater than that of physical blows—is a common theme in Singer's stories. It is given unusually dramatic expression in "Henne Fire" (*The Séance*), the story of a woman who spews fire and vitriol with such regularity that her nickname reflects her neighbors' suspicion that she is not a human being at all, but an escapee from Gehenna, the pit of hell. Swearing is her normal discourse. When it drives away her four children and her husband, she curses her neighbors and blasphemes against God. The incendiary power of her wicked tongue is literally realized; but the demons it lets loose turn against their creator: "Henne's bed linen began to burn of itself. . . . Henne sent everybody to the devil; and now the devil had turned on her" (140). The homeless

Henne is offered shelter by merciful neighbors, but so thoroughly has her fiery tongue permeated her being that she has only to enter a dwelling—even the rabbi's *succah* (tabernacle)—to set it ablaze. Finally, and it would seem inevitably, Henne is self-consumed; her blackened skeleton is found in a chair: "Henne had been burned to a crisp. But how? . . . For a person to be so totally consumed, you'd need a fire bigger than the one in the bathhouse on Fridays. . . . [T]he chair was untouched. . . . Yet Henne was one piece of coal" (146). Death by spontaneous combustion is the appropriate punishment for one who all her life had used the word *fire* in her curses, wishing upon her enemies fire in the head and belly, fever in all their limbs. There is a double moral here: first, that fiery hatred, pursued long enough, burns up the hater herself; and second, that "words have power. The proverb says: 'A blow passes, but a word remains' " (147).

Singer's almost-superstitious conviction of the permanence of words (and therefore of the need for extreme caution in choosing and speaking them) supplies the motive for "The Plagiarist" (*The Seance*). Rabbi Kasriel Dan Kinsker discovers that one of his disciples, Shabsai Getsel, has copied whole selections of the rabbi's manuscripts and printed them under his own name. The rabbi reacts with restraint, especially when he recalls the warning against shaming someone, even a sinner, in public. It is only when his wife points out that the plagiarist and not their son is going to be appointed assistant rabbi that Reb Kasriel Dan succumbs to his resentment of the young man who wants to take everything from him: "Involuntarily something within Reb Kasriel Dan cried out, 'He'll not live to see the day.' But he immediately remembered that it is forbidden to curse anyone, even in thought" (102). So much does the old rabbi regret his momentary transgression that he burns his manuscripts lest, after his death, Shabsai Getsel be discovered and shamed. After all, "the main thing was that the commentaries were published and would be studied. In heaven the truth was known" (105).

But in Singer's moral tales it is axiomatic that a curse, once uttered (even silently), cannot be undone. Shabsai Getsel, Reb Kasriel learns, is critically ill; and it is irresistibly clear to him that his involuntary curse is to blame. Recalling the proverb that "to punish the just is not good," he accepts the rabbinic interpretation of the verse as meaning "nor is it proper for the righteous to mete out punishment" (108). Such an interpretation itself requires interpretation. Can it be that only the *un*righteous are fitted to mete out punishment? Or does it propose that the patterns of guilt and punishment are so complexly intertwined that violence does even justice unjustly?

At any rate, when Shabsai Getsel dies, Reb Kasriel Dan has no doubt that he is responsible for the plagiarist's death. Indeed, the crime of plagiarism has, by the story's end, become trivial, insignificant, forgotten—displaced in the consciousness of the reader as well as that of Reb Kasriel Dan by the greater crime, or rather sin (momentary though it was), of involuntarily cursing someone. Reb Kasriel Dan decides to go into exile to do penance for his sin, which is nothing less than murder, because "the Commandment 'Thou shalt not kill' includes all sins" (110). The magnification of a momentary lapse—Reb Kasriel Dan's curse—into the most dreadful of sins shows how for Singer the secular writer his father's insistence that nothing is neutral, that you always did either a good deed or a sin, remained a compelling idea.

This story, in which a bad deed proves more potent than good intentions, also offers a curious negative complement to those in which Singer stresses that good deeds are more important than firm belief and pure intention. In "A Piece of Advice" (*The Spinoza of Market Street*) a *misnagid* (opponent of Hasidism) who suffers from a bad temper resorts to a Hasidic rabbi for a cure for his raging anger and receives a prescription for eight days of flattery of everyone he meets. If you are not pious, says the rabbi, pretend that you are: "The Almighty does not require good intentions. The deed is what counts. It is what you do that matters. Are you angry perhaps? Go ahead and be angry, but speak gentle words and be friendly at the same time. Are you afraid of being a dissembler? So what if you pretend to be something you aren't? For whose sake are you lying? For your Father in Heaven. His Holy Name, blessed be He, knows the intention, and the intention behind the intention, and it is this that is the main thing" (142). Intention is ephemeral, evanescent, personal; under the aspect of eternity, it counts for little in the moral order of the universe. God registers actions, the true indicators of faith, and not intentions.

But the story teaches that the ethical act that affects the moral order also conduces to individual well-being and converges with faith. If you act ethically despite raging bad intentions, you may in time come to like being ethical, and do the deed more willingly and "naturally." Gradually, this angry man *becomes* good-natured, and then enunciates for his disciples the lesson he has learned: "If you can't be a good Jew, act the good Jew, because if you act something, you *are* it." Ceasing to do wrong things antecedes the obliteration of the desire to do them. Moreover, what holds true for ethical action holds true for faith as well: "If you are in despair, act as though you believed. Faith will come afterwards" (144).

It is worth remarking that "A Piece of Advice," which might serve as a paradigm of Singer's moral tales, is similar to I. L. Peretz's famous story "If Not Higher." There, too, a skeptical anti-Hasid is "converted" to Hasidism because he is witness to its moral efficacy; Hasidism triumphs on pragmatic rather than strictly "religious" grounds. Singer is more prone than Peretz to turn the message of Hasidism into swallowable pellets of intellection and "advice," but he follows the older writer in admiring the moral efficacy of a faith he could not share. Singer's ethical tales are profoundly skeptical of new, secular faiths. In "The Bishop's Robe" (*A Crown of Feathers*) he depicts spiritualism as a form of of fakery that leads to promiscuity, emptiness, and suicide. "On a Wagon," in the same volume, shows that "enlightened" Judaism is a halfway house on the road to worldliness and—again—promiscuity. Singer's father was only half-right in blaming "secular writers like Peretz" for leading the Jews to heresy. Singer followed Peretz in singing the praises of Hasidism for its joy, for its openness to the Jewish masses, above all for its moral efficacy; but he was also like Peretz in that he could say nearly everything in favor of Hasidism except that it is true. However moved we may be by Singer's moral tales, however impressed by the moral position they enforce, we may yet ask whether the utility of religion is any less open to debate than its truth.

Archetypal Tales:
Memory and Survival

Singer has often said that amnesia is the only sickness from which Jews do not suffer. By this he means not only that Jews remember what happened in their own lifetime but that their memory stretches back through the collective experience of their people, all the way back to its origins at Sinai. A recurrent scene in his fiction is the night of Tisha B'Av (Ninth of Av), when, according to the Talmud, Jews mourn the "disasters that recurred again and again to the Jewish people," although in fact only the fall of Betar, the last stronghold of Bar Kokhba captured by the Romans in 135 c.e., occurred on that day. The destruction of the First Temple and all subsequent major catastrophes that happened at about that time were gradually subsumed by that day. These catastrophes came to include the destruction of the Second Temple, the decree against the entrance of the children of Israel into the Holy Land after the incident of the Twelve Spies, the plowing up of Jerusalem in 136 c.e., and the Expulsion of the Jews from Spain in 1492. In recent years, some have argued that the Holocaust, the destruction of European Jewry, should also be commemorated on the very same ninth day of Av.

The gentile Dr. Yaretzky in Singer's "The Shadow of a Crib" (*The Spinoza of Market Street*) observes that although the Jews "dwell side by side with us, . . . spiritually they are somewhere in Palestine, on Mount Sinai or God knows where." The reason for this double life of the Jews, so he has heard, is that "the Jews do not record their history, they have no sense of chronology. . . . [I]nstinctively they know that time and space are mere illusion" (77). Dr. Yaretzky's observations have been confirmed by the historian Yosef Hayim Yerushalmi in his recent study of Jewish history and Jewish memory. "Only in Israel and nowhere else," he writes, "is the injunction to remember felt as a religious imperative to an entire people. . . . 'Remember the days of old, consider the years of ages past' (Deut. 32:7). . . . 'Remember what Amalek did to you' (Deut. 25:17). . . . And, with a hammering

28

insistence: 'Remember that you were a slave in Egypt' "[15] But the powerful Jewish sense of memory was not, and is not, the same as a powerful sense of history. Indeed, Yerushalmi points out that even though memory of the past was a central element of Jewish experience, the sense of history was peripheral, the need for historians barely recognized. Singer is the poet laureate of a Jewish sense of the past that is archetypal and circular rather than historical and linear. His narratives touching on the Holocaust, for example, tend to view the Nazis as only the latest in the long succession of those murderous outsiders who have obtruded themselves upon Jewish history again and again. "Yes," sighs the narrator of *The Family Moskat*, "every generation had its Pharoahs and Hamans and Chmielnickis. Now it was Hitler" (578).

In 1933 Singer published the first of what might be called miracle tales—stories that celebrate Jewish survival and, by taking for granted the timelessness of biblical archetypes, declare that Jews, throughout their long history, have never really changed. "The Old Man" (*Gimpel the Fool*)[16] tells the tale of the nonagenarian Reb Moshe Ber, who has managed, but only barely, to survive both his children and his grand-children. He had come to Warsaw from Jozefow just before the outbreak of the Great War, to live with his prosperous son. But two years later, the war ravaged the family, leaving only the old man, who must now retrace his steps and return to his Turisk Hasidim in Jozefow.

Enduring intense cold and almost unrelieved hunger, even convinced at times that he is already dead, the ancient Moshe Ber makes his way by foot across war-torn Europe, through Galicia, Zamosc, Bilgoray, and finally back to the home he had left. Nothing in the narrative of his suffering and deprivation and ultimate rescue departs from surface realism, even naturalism: yet the story culminates in a miracle, one that is taken entirely for granted by the old man. The Turisk Hasidim, almost at a loss to know how to express their gratitude for his safe return to them, arrange Moshe Ber's marriage to a forty-year-old, deaf-and-dumb village girl. "Exactly nine months later she gave birth to a son—now he had someone to say *kaddish* for him." With perfect self-possession, Moshe Ber names the child Isaac, reveals that he is now a hundred years old, and reminds his friends that the miracle of Jewish survival is as real and living as it ever was: " 'And Abraham was a hundred years old,' he recited, 'when his son Isaac was born unto him. And Sarah said: "God hath made me laugh so that all who hear will laugh with me" ' " (159). The meaning of the whole story bursts forth in its stunning conclusion. Those present at the miracle laugh not merely because of the age of Moshe Ber-Abraham, but at the sheer madness of the Jewish faith that, despite all catastrophe, despite the destruction of millions of individuals, the Jewish *people* will live.

"Two Markets" (*Passions*) is another tale that moves effortlessly from realism into miracle and thereby asserts permanence over change. The narrator begins with a vivid and detailed description of the street market on Krochmalna Street in Warsaw. At the center of the picture is a hunchbacked fruit dealer whose wit, aggressiveness, and disfigurement had fascinated the young Singer. In the second part of the tale, Singer is an old man in the ostensibly new world of Tel Aviv, where he is walking with his Hebrew translator. He complains (in a manner typical of American Jews whose vision does not penetrate surfaces) that the center of Tel Aviv is indistinguishable from New York: "Pointing to the large square, I asked, 'In what way is this the land of Israel? If it were not for the Hebrew signs it could just as well be Brooklyn—the same buses, the same noise, the same stench of gasoline, the same movie houses. Modern civilization wipes out all individuality. I foresee that if life is discovered on the planet Mars, we will soon have—' " (229).

But reality, acting as a severe schoolmaster, cuts short this description of life on Mars by confronting Singer with Krochmalna Street. In the center of Tel Aviv, Singer comes upon a narrow street crowded with fruit and vegetable stands, reeking of familiar odors, resonant with familiar voices. "For a moment I imagined that the hustlers were shouting out their merchandise in Warsaw Yiddish, but I soon realized that it was Hebrew" (229).

As he makes his way through the Carmel Market, Singer experiences "a second miracle": he sees the hunchback, "so like the one in Warsaw that for an instant I thought it was he" (229). If not he, perhaps it was a son or grandson (if the condition is hereditary). The hunchback even gets into an altercation with the police, precisely like those in which his Warsaw "ancestor" was habitually involved.

In discovering himself to be simultaneously in the Land of Israel and in old Warsaw, Singer appears to offer support to the Zionist claim that only in Israel can the Jews hope to recover the culture and inner world that was destroyed in Europe. This idea of restoration and resurrection in the Land of Israel is also embedded in Jewish imagination going back to a time long before political Zionism existed. In the

Talmud (Megillah 29a) we read that "the synagogues and houses of learning in Babylon will in time to come be planted in Eretz Israel." If the synagogues and study houses, then why not the fruit and vegetable markets and the peddlers too?

But even the Zionist motif remains subservient to Singer's conviction that all Jewish experience is a reenactment of biblical archetypes. He catches his translator, "absorbed in the ancient feminine lust for bargains," fancying a pair of black velvet panties and urges her to buy them because—so he assures her—"these panties were worn by the Queen of Sheba when King Solomon solved all her riddles and she showed him all her treasures" (233).

"The Little Shoemakers" (*Gimpel the Fool*) is one of Singer's most beautiful stories and also one of his most ambitious. At once a mourning over what has been lost and a celebration of what has survived, it tries to encompass within a few pages the enormous upheavals that have gripped the Jews in modern times. Irving Howe says that this story "sums up the whole of contemporary Jewish experience: from tradition to modernity, from the old country to the new, from the ghetto to the camps."[17] Perhaps because it treats events that defy credibility and have almost always proved resistant to naturalistic representation, the story comes much closer to the formal devices of archetype and allegory than most of Singer's tales do. It thus collapses the most cataclysmic historical events—pogroms, mass migrations of unprecedented magnitude, the Holocaust—into the fable of three generations of a single family transplanted from a shtetl of Eastern Europe to the new world of the United States.

Like many of Singer's tales, "The Little Shoemakers" commences in the aftermath of Chmielnitzki's pogroms in the seventeenth century. But it moves quickly to modern times and to Abba, who, like his ancestors, is a righteous shoemaker (and whose surname—Shuster—gives his occupation). Abba lives his life in Frampol within the traditional bounds of Jewish faith. His learning is wholly religious and completely unmediated by a sense of historical distance. He can identify with Noah, still more with Abraham. Indeed, "he often thought that if the Almighty were to call on him to sacrifice his eldest son, Gimpel, he would rise early in the morning and carry out his commands without delay." Abba believes that he, like all the Jews since the destruction of the Second Temple, lives in exile, far from the homeland in Eretz Israel, because he has sinned, and not because God has been unfaithful or powerless. But Abba is sustained in exile by his knowledge of the unbroken continuity between himself and the Patriarchs—"as if he too were part of the Bible" (93). This apparently fantastic belief is thoroughly confirmed by the biblical magnitude of the events through which Abba, like all the Jews of Europe, is destined to live. These are indeed biblical times.

But although he awaits the Redemption, and will be ready to leave for the Holy Land when the Messiah comes, Abba's attachments to the place where he lives in exile are as intricate and traditional as we might expect them to be in a people who, like the Jews, had lived in Poland for eight hundred years. Though his house is in bad repair, he resists the recommendation of his wife, Pesha, to tear it down and build a new one. He would rather keep things as they are, because he "found it hard to part with the home in which his parents and grand-parents, and the whole family, stretching back for generations, had lived and died." Abba understands that the fullness of life is an ac-cumulation of memories, preserved to us by material objects, appar-ently dead yet resonant with the life of the past: "The walls were like an album in which the fortunes of the family had been recorded." The Book of Memory is almost as sacred to Abba as the Five Books of Moses. No, he decides, "there was nothing to change. Let everything stand as it had stood for ages" (98–99).

But Abba is unable to transmit either his wisdom or his contentment to his sons. No sooner has he made his commitment to standing still than his son Gimpel announces his intention to go to America. Gimpel wants enlightenment and American plumbing, both of which are in short supply in Frampol. Although Gimpel's parting is bitter, the tone of his letters from America is conciliatory—and satisfied as well. He proudly reports that there, unlike in Poland, "no one walks with his eyes on the ground, everybody holds his head high" (103). Gimpel induces his brother Getzel to follow him, Getzel brings over Treitel, and so on, until all seven brothers have left—seven Jews of the ap-proximately two million who, during four decades, beginning in the 1880s, came from Eastern Europe to the United States. But Abba and his wife, Pesha, though bereft of their sons, can see no reason to move from one corner of the Diaspora to another, more alien one.

For forty years, during which time he loses Pesha, Abba resists the pleadings of his sons to join them in America, and consoles himself with work at the shoemaker's bench. But the next upheaval in the life of Eastern European Jewry sweeps even Abba away from his traditional moorings. As Hitler's barbarians descend upon Poland, Abba assumes that the deliverance from exile, so long delayed, is finally at hand: "One morning, while Abba was wandering among his thoughts, he heard a tremendous crash. The old man shook in his bones: the blast of the Messiah's trumpet. He dropped the boot he had been working on and ran out in ecstasy. But it was not Elijah the Prophet proclaiming the Messiah. Nazi planes were bombing Frampol" (108). Abba, like the Patriarchs, is indeed living in biblical times, but the only Messiah, as Hertz Yanovar insists at the end of *The Family Moskat*, is death. Abba, who from his youth had, like Abraham, been ready to heed the command to get out of his country, now does indeed abandon the house of his forefathers and the place of his birth, just as Abraham had done; only he does so not at the behest of God, but to save his life.

The fifth part of "The Little Shoemakers" stresses more insistently than any other the degree to which the utterly incredible things that have befallen the Jews in the past century resemble the fantastic tales of the Bible. In a few months Abba relives the experiences of Abraham, Jacob, and Jonah, and follows his ancestors through Sodom and Gomorrah, Beth-El, and the belly of the whale. Intimations of archetypal experiences haunt every moment of first his escape to Romania and then his voyage across the ocean: "Abba had little learning, but Biblical references ran through his mind" (112). Destruction, exile, and flight are the inescapable matrix of Jewish historical experience, so that "Abba felt he had become his own great-great-grandfather, who had fled Chmielnitzki's pogroms" (110).

Abba's Jonah-like trip across the Atlantic has been arranged by his prosperous sons, who live in suburban New Jersey. The sons have, after a fashion, continued the fifteen-generations-old family tradition by operating a shoe factory. They are also, after a fashion, Jews, but are so clean shaven, so sterilized, so "reformed" that when he is brought to their synagogue, "Abba was sure he had been hauled into church to be converted." Abba's traumatic experiences make it hard for him to fathom that he is in New Jersey rather than the Land of Goshen. His sons and daughters-in-law nearly despair of rescuing him from the nightmare of the Jewish past, until he accidentally comes upon a sack containing his shoemaker's equipment from Frampol. Work, which provides the one unfailing continuity in his life, proves to be his salvation. Once his sons provide him with a cobbler's bench and the tools of his craft, Abba returns to life.

For all Singer's wry condescension toward the Americanized imitation of the Jewish world of Eastern Europe (itself an imitation of the

Holy Land), he does show the community reestablished in this new world: "On the following Sunday eight work stools were set up in the hut. Abba's sons spread sackcloth aprons on their knees and went to work, cutting soles and shaping heels, boring holes and hammering pegs, as in the good old days." "The Little Shoemakers" is one of the few Singer stories to allow for the possibility of a collective Jewish identity in the United States, for Abba and his sons survive not merely as individuals, but as a Jewish community: "No, praise God, they had not become idolators in Egypt. They had not forgotten their heritage, nor had they lost themselves among the unworthy" (118–119). The lyrical rise of the story's end is a hymn to the Jewish power of survival which gains its special force from the fact that it is built into an elegy over a destroyed civilization.

Singer's archetypal tales of Jewish survival, especially those which, while taking into account the terrible catastrophes that have befallen the Jews, reach back to the special destiny conferred upon them at Sinai, declare that a nation that has been dying for thousands of years is a living nation. Is there any greater paradox than the fact that the first ancient non-Jewish document to mention Israel by name is the gloating report of Mer-neptah, king of Egypt, in 1215 B.C.E., that "Israel is desolated; its seed is no more"? No one has articulated that paradox better than Simon Rawidowicz: "As far as historical reality is concerned, we are confronted here with a phenomenon which has almost no parallel in mankind's story: a nation that has been disappearing constantly for the last two thousand years, exterminated in dozens of lands all over the globe, reduced to half or third of its population by tyrants ancient and modern—and yet it still exists, falls and rises, loses all its possessions and re-equips itself for a new start, a second, a third chance—always fearing the end, never afraid to make a new beginning."[18]

Singer's stories of Jewish survival propose that the reason this "historical reality" has no parallel is that it is not so much a historical fact as superhistorical truth.

Tales of Apocalypse
and Politics

The sense of an intimate and mystical connection between destruction and rebirth is deeply embedded in Jewish sacred literature and historical consciousness. In the book of Ezekiel, the prospect that God will make "a full end of the remnant of Israel" is inseparable from the promise that "I will even gather you from the peoples, and assemble you out of the countries where ye have been scattered, and I will give you the land of Israel" (Ezek. 11:13, 16). The legend that the Messiah was born on the very day that the Temple was destroyed is contained in a midrash (homily) (Lam. Rab. 1) and is deeply embedded in Jewish tradition, as is the Talmudic notion that the Messiah will come only in a generation totally innocent or wholly guilty.

The relation between the religious idea of redemption through catastrophe and particular historical events can be grotesque and shocking. Long before 1492, Cabalistic writers selected that year as the one in which catastrophe would bring the redemption of the Jews. The catastrophe came, to be sure, in the form of expulsion from Spain; but where was the redemption? In the seventeenth century the horrendous massacres of Jews perpetrated by the Ukrainian cossack revolutionary Chmielnitzki—massacres that are as immediate to Singer's imagination as the Holocaust—led a large segment of the Jewish world to attach itself to the messianism of Sabbatai Zevi out of a desperate desire to fathom the catastrophe that had occurred as the antecedent to an apocalyptic revelation. But the plunge into Sabbatean mysticism led to a Jewish catastrophe of immorality and apostasy nearly as horrendous as the one it purported to explain.

Unlike most Yiddish writers, Singer has been powerfully (though not always sympathetically) attracted to the tradition of "false messianism" in Judaism, especially to the tradition of the false Messiah Sabbatai Zevi. His fullest treatment of it is in the novel *Satan in Goray*,[19] but it exercises a strong if often indirect influence on many of his other works. Singer links this tradition with political as well as religious utopianism; and he takes utopianism to be a dangerous human impulse that is just as likely to express hatred of the human race as love of it. The utopian impatience with human and social imperfection too often leads to the desire to force an end to the world as we know it, in the belief that only out of chaos can a new cosmos arise. "To me," Singer has said, "Sabbatai Zevi was the symbol of the man who tries to do good and comes out bad. . . . [He] is in a way Stalin and all these people who tried so hard to create a better world and who ended up by creating the greatest misery."[20]

The typical elements of Singer's apocalyptic tales are the following: impatience to escape from a desperate situation; eager responsiveness to someone (a gentleman-devil or messianic disciple) offering release from the prohibitions of rabbinic law; the lure of eroticism; and the desire to turn things upside down. But the results of rebellion against the moral law and the boring imperfections of quotidian existence are not always unqualified disaster. The range of possibilities and perhaps even some degree of ambiguity in Singer's negative judgment of messianism may be seen in "The Gentleman from Cracow" and "The Destruction of Kreshev."

"The Gentleman from Cracow" [*Gimpel the Fool*] is, on the surface, an un-ironic morality tale unimpeachably based on a "parchment chronicle" signed by "trustworthy witnesses." The town of Frampol, beset by poverty and drought, is tempted into gross transgressions of the law to obtain the gold that the wealthy newcomer, allegedly a doctor from Cracow, has brought. When he suggests so un-Jewish an activity as a ball, Rabbi Ozer warns his flock that they are being led astray by the Evil One. But the wisdom of the Torah can no longer penetrate the skulls of young men thinking only of the ball and of the women to be seen there. At the ball, the Croesus from Cracow offers to enrich the whole community on the condition that, by lottery, every girl provide herself with a husband before midnight. He himself, in accordance with the Cinderella pattern of the story, draws a lascivious harlot named Hodle. She, like a number of similar women in Singer's fictional world, has sinned throughout her life, and not for bread, but "for the sheer pleasure." The specifically anti-Jewish character of sexual promiscuity and excess is emphasized by the groom's blasphemous parody of the formula recited to the bride during a Jewish marriage ceremony: "With this ring, be thou desecrated to me according to the blasphemy of Korah and Ishmael" (38–39).

Only one person present at this festival of abominations sees what it portends. He is an old man who warns the Jews of the wrath to come: "A fire is upon us, burning, Jews, Satan's fire. Save your souls, Jews. Flee, before it is too late!" (38). But he is treated like most bearers of ill tidings to the Jews: he is gagged and expelled—and proved correct.[21] Hardly has he left the scene when a bolt of lightning strikes the study house, the ritual bath, and the synagogue simultaneously, setting the whole town on fire. Having witnessed all this, even the townspeople of Frampol can hardly be surprised when the gentleman from Cracow reveals himself to be the Chief of the Devils, Ketev Mriri, and his bride turns out to be Lilith.

All of Frampol, except for the rabbi's house, is consumed by fire, and most of the inhabitants find themselves naked and floundering in mud, a fitting symbol of the sexual excess in which they have been mired. As is so often the case in Singer's works, the desire for a radical transformation of one's state leads downward toward the animal rather than upward toward the angelic: " 'Jews, for the sake of God, save your souls! You are in the hands of Satan!' But the townspeople, too entranced to heed his cries, continued their frenzied movements for a long time, jumping like frogs, shaking as though with fever. With hair uncovered and breasts bare, the women laughed, cried, and swayed. . . . Old men and women were immersed in slime up to their loins. They scarcely looked alive" (41). Yet the rabbi's passionate exhortations to resist evil and his courageous offer of himself as a scapegoat for the community's sins do have their effect, and only one among the great multitude of sinners loses his life. Nevertheless, great loss of life there is, for, as usual, it is the innocent and not the guilty who suffer. In a passage that echoes *The Family Moskat*'s reproach to Jews who lead their own children to the slaughterhouse, the narrator reveals that "it was the infants who had been the real victims of the passion for gold that had caused the inhabitants of Frampol to transgress. The infants' cribs were burned, their little bones were charred" (43). This is an especially painful punishment for the people of Frampol because, throughout their years of wretched poverty and endless bad fortune, they had always "been blessed with fine children" (24).

But the catastrophe brings in its wake more than punishment and makes of "The Gentleman from Cracow" something other than a moral tale. The fire proves to be an apocalyptic event, the massacre of the innocent children a prelude to Frampol's entry into a better way of life, even a new world. The paradoxical outcome of so much greed, lust, and blasphemy is compassion, charity, diligence, cooperation, and reconstruction—all of which had been little in evidence before the arrival of the gentleman-devil from Cracow. The lust for gold is permanently stifled: "From generation to generation the people remained paupers. A gold coin became an abomination in Frampol, and even silver was looked at askance" (44). This is one of Singer's apocalyptic tales in which the dangerous theory that "worse is better" is belatedly vindicated. True, the vindication comes at a very high price, one that might well prompt the question of why so great a conflagration is required to teach so small a lesson. Do you have to fall into the Grand Canyon to believe that it really is deep? On the other hand, one might argue that the story's paradoxical relation between evil and good serves (in a further irony) to confirm the traditional theology that holds that out of evil must come good, and that even the most enterprising of devils is a servant of heaven.

"The Destruction of Kreshev" (*The Spinoza of Market Street*) may be viewed as a pendant or counterpoint to "The Gentleman from Cracow" among Singer's tales in the apocalyptic mode. For this story, narrated by Satan himself, is an oblique but harsh criticism of the apocalyptic temper, and particularly the belief that "worse is better," that the path to virtue is paved with excess, and that catastrophe is the necessary antecedent to messianic redemption. Here too (as in so many Singer stories of every mode and voice) it is sex that both precipitates and contains within itself all other sins; and here too it is the innocent children of the town who are the primary victims of the lust of their elders. But "The Destruction of Kreshev," like *Satan in Goray*, does not encourage us to rest in the comforting paradox that out of evil comes good, out of defilement, purity, out of wickedness, redemption.

Whereas the gentleman from Cracow involves a whole community in sin, the chief sinners in Kreshev are distinct individuals whose careers are traced for us in some detail before they take their plunge into perversion and defilement. Lise, the central figure of the tale, bears some resemblance to the heroine of "Yentl the Yeshiva Boy," for she can hardly bake a potato but is as adept as the cleverest man in the study of Scripture and Talmud. Her other peculiarity is an excess of modesty. When her father, Reb Bunim—a wealthy, virtuous, and sweet-tempered man—asks her (at age fifteen) to choose between two prospective husbands, a tall, handsome, rich man from Lublin who is a mediocre scholar, and an undersized and homely Talmudic prodigy from Warsaw, her intellectualism and her prudishness direct her to the latter. This miracle of erudition, whose name is Shloimele, dazzles the

Kreshev Jews with his intellectual pyrotechnics. Readers of Yiddish literature will recognize him as a blood brother to Peretz's Chananiah, who in the great story "Devotion without End" epitomizes the false scholars who come to the Torah "not for its own sake or from love of God but out of a lust to shine in their own right." Singer chooses to associate this peculiarly Jewish lust with another, more generally available kind.

Once they are married, the clever Shloimele lures his loving wife into the study of Cabala, into sexual research and experimentation, into animalism. It is specifically his intellectualism that is responsible for an impotence that can only be assuaged by imaginings of infidelity and perversion. The dedication to evil of this Talmudic scholar is, however, of the most high-minded sort, for he is a disciple of the long-dead false Messiah Sabbatai Zevi, and shares his master's belief that an excess of degradation means greater sanctity, and the more heinous the wickedness, the closer the day of redemption: "Since this generation cannot become completely pure, let it grow completely impure!" (191). His own plunge into the abyss is justified as the necessary prelude to sublimity, his energetic devotion to sin as the means of burning through all those passions which must be consummated before the Messiah can come. Just as his master Sabbatai Zevi had converted to Islam in order (so his dutiful followers believed) to go into that pit of defilement from which the divine sparks had to be rescued, so does Shloimele threaten to convert to Roman Catholicism.

The instrument for Shloimele's realization of his perverse ambitions is the coachman Mendel. Mendel, like many Jews before and since, has chosen to become Esau and to forsake his own heritage. He completely disregards Jewish laws and customs, dedicates himself to lechery, and espouses a wholly materialistic view of life that pays no heed to threats of what may await him in the world to come. Shloimele forces Lise into adultery with Mendel after persuading her that she and the coachman are reincarnations of, respectively, Abishag the Shunammite, and Adonijah, the son of Haggith. Lise's ruination, we are again reminded by the satanic narrator, is caused by her husband's overdeveloped intellect: "In truth, Shloimele, the villain, devised this whim merely to satisfy his own depraved passions, since he had grown perverse from too much thinking" (197). Unlike the stories in which what Morris Golden[22] calls the Spinoza theme is dominant and the flatulent, dyspeptic thinker (e.g., Dr. Fischelson, the "Spinoza of Market Street") must be cured of his cerebral illness by sexual union with an unintellectual female, "The Destruction of Kreshev" makes intellectual imbalance the immediate cause of sexual depravity.

At the point of his most intense eagerness to break out of the old world into the new, regardless of the price to be paid in mere "temporal" affliction, Shloimele has said: "I love fire! I love a holocaust. . . . I would like the whole world to burn" (192). When the abominations of Shloimele, Lise, and Mendel are made public, the town's rabbi declares that he is in truth not the rabbi of Kreshev but of Sodom and Gomorrah, the biblical cities that were destroyed by fire from above because all their inhabitants had become wicked. But the analogy is inexact. Kreshev's abominations have been committed only by three people, but even after Mendel is punished and Lise hangs herself, the town and its inhabitants are destroyed by fire and plague. The holocaust beloved of apocalyptic desperadoes does indeed materialize, but the promised redemption is nowhere in evidence at the end of the tale. If, in "The Gentleman from Cracow," Singer has paid grudging respect to the good that may sometimes result from demonic energy, here he reasserts his more characteristic suspicion of false messianism in its multifarious forms.

The most common form of the messianic delusion in the twentieth century, especially among Jews, has been political rather than religious. Singer's fiction is full of people who succumb to the utopian blandishments of left-wing political systems. His do-gooders are an objectionable bunch because they confuse doing good with feeling good about what they are doing, which is a very different thing; and they end by doing mischief and evil to everybody, including themselves. Some of Singer's strong feeling on this subject derives from personal experience. He was alienated from the Yiddish literary world, for example, partly by the dogged loyalty of many Yiddish leftists to Stalin. The narrator of "Advice" (*The Image*)[23] notes how even after the whole world knew that Stalin had murdered most of the Yiddish writers in Russia, "the Communist Yiddish newspaper in New York assured its readers that all these accusations came from enemies of the people, the lackeys of Fascism" (7). Singer long harbored bitterness toward his Communist mistress Runia. In the story called "The Son" (*A Friend of Kafka*) he recalls how their child "was five years old when I parted with his mother. I went to America, she to Soviet Russia. But apparently one revolution was not enough for her. She wanted the 'permanent revolution.' And they would have liquidated her in Moscow if she hadn't had someone who could reach the ear of a high official" (246). Decades after their parting in 1935, Singer would generalize from his own experience with Runia and other Jewish leftists: "When I was young, I already saw the bad results of all these good deeds. I have seen young people go to Soviet Russia and disappear there. All these illusions and all these vain hopes. I compared them to the people who believed in Sabbatai Zevi" (Singer/Howe, 36–37).

But Singer's skepticism about high-minded political activism is too profound and pervasive to be reduced to a private grudge. We can feel his presence just behind the mask of such characters as Professor Vladimir Eibeschutz in "Pigeons" (*A Friend of Kafka*). Eibeschutz is a professor of history who leaves Warsaw University "not only because of the anti-Semitic students but also because of the Jewish Communist students who used the Jew-baiting of the others for their own propaganda purposes" (115–16). Eibeschutz shares with his creator not only the habit of feeding the neighborhood pigeons but the conviction that history is made by the wicked, and the wicked are always the same, interchangeable with one another: "Villains cannot rest. Whether it be war or revolution, whether they fight under one flag or another, no matter what their slogan, their aim remains the same—to perpetrate evil, cause pain, shed blood. One common aim united Alexander of Macedonia and Hamilcar, Genghis Khan and Charlemagne, Chmielnitzki and Napoleon, Robespierre and Lenin" (121). History, as we noted earlier, doesn't really exist for Singer (since all things are held to repeat themselves), but study of the past keeps reminding him of the Yiddish proverb "So many Hamans, only one Purim."

In Singer's fiction the Jewish leftist is usually someone who strives for the emancipation of every people except his own and for the abolition of all privileges—except his own. An Israeli woman in "The Mentor" (*A Friend of Kafka*) describes how the modern Jew "has to bleed for humanity—battle the reactionaries, worry about the Chinese, the Manchurians, the Russians, the untouchables in India, the Negroes in America. He preaches revolution and at the same time he wants all the privileges of capitalism for himself" (101–2). A good example of this, although he is treated with pity more than anger, is Maurice, an anarchist, in the story "Property" (*A Crown of Feathers*). In his youth, in the 1890s, he "believed only in terror," deriding those anarchists who put their reliance on propaganda. He would make a special effort to *épater les Juifs* by organizing an annual Yom Kippur (Day of Atonement) ball, where it was considered obligatory "to eat non-kosher food, preferably pork, just to annoy the Almighty," who, however, in the view of all advanced leftist thinkers, did not exist. Maurice's apartment was adorned by a sign proclaiming that "PROPERTY IS THEFT." Eventually he and his wife moved to a commune in Oregon, which soon disintegrated because each resident utopian "had his own ideas not only about how to liberate humanity but also about how to stack hay and milk cows" (88). When Singer's interlocutor, who has been telling him Maurice's story, next sees the anticapitalist anarchist, he is a slumlord in Miami; and the first of his three wives is "already in what we all tried to make—a better world" (91).

Singer's gloomy view of politics—especially idealistic politics—is that it is a violation of the first commandment. "My idol," says a character in "The Egotist" (*A Crown of Feathers*), "was the Revolution, and therefore I am punished by God" (273). But Singer also rejects political activity on stoical or what he has called Buddhist grounds, that is, that "the best thing you can do is run away from evil, not fight it, because the moment you begin to fight evil, you become a part of evil yourself" (Singer/Howe, 36). The fear of corrupting oneself to evil in the very act of combating it flits through Singer's stories. We have already seen how in "The Magazine" (*A Crown of Feathers*) Singer recalls his conversation with a writer who aspired to save the world through a "little magazine":

> "The trouble is that the wicked make all the noise and the just sleep."
> "They'll always sleep," I said.
> "They can be woken up."
> "If they're woken up, they'll become wicked." (175)

Singer's quietism in relation to politics arises from his conviction that attempts to resolve the anomalies and injustices of society through revolutionary action will bring far worse anomalies and injustices than already exist. He remembers obsessively that Stalin and Hitler were the two most potent revolutionaries of this century and that both proved to be false messiahs. If we then ask what advice Singer might offer to a young person seeking to reform society, it would be that which Thomas Carlyle gave to a would-be world-betterer: "Make an honest man of yourself, and there will be one rascal less in Scotland."

Stories of Faith and Doubt

In his interviews, Singer has consistently represented himself as one who believes in God, providence, and design, but not at all in revelation and only very slightly in "evidences" of God's existence and goodness. That God is good and not malicious is, he has said, certain, yet the great disparity between human and divine intelligence makes it difficult for human beings to recognize the supernatural concern for their well-being. He alleges all "dogmas" to be the work of human beings and not truths that emanated from a realm beyond the human. That is why he has cast off the yoke of rabbinic Judaism and the observance and self-discipline it entails. But the spiritual reach of his short stories, a reach that takes Singer well beyond the limits of his realistic and naturalistic contemporaries, derives mainly from his openness to the supernatural: "The higher Powers, I am convinced, are always with us, at every moment, everywhere, except, perhaps, at the meetings of Marxists and other left-wingers. There is no God there; they have passed a motion to that effect" (Blocker/Elman, 372).

Occasionally, as in "Sabbath in Portugal" (*Passions*), Singer will express some guilt about his desertion of the traditions in which he was raised. In this tale the author, while on a visit to Portugal, receives princely hospitality from a Portuguese host who believes himself descended from Marranos, the Jews who had, centuries earlier, accepted Christianity outwardly but continued to practice Judaism in secret. Invited to a vegetarian meal on the Sabbath, the narrator is disturbed to find that "the Sabbath I had desecrated for years had caught up with me in a Gentile home in Lisbon" (84). This recognition that he has casually dispensed with what other Jews have for centuries suffered to retain proves fleeting, however, and the opportunity for self-criticism is wasted in a surge of nostalgia as the narrator convinces himself that the hostess is actually his first love, who had been shot by the Nazis. The story does, though only in passing, make one "theological" point, namely, that the state of Israel, which to the superficial eye may appear to be peopled by large numbers of "secularists," has a profound religious significance: "How is it," asks Singer's Marrano host, "that so many nations vanished and Jews still lived to return to their land? Doesn't it prove the Bible is true?" (86).

This kind of general reflection on whether the course of Jewish history confirms or denies the existence of God and the truth of biblical prophecy is rarely at the center of Singer's stories about religious faith, which deal primarily with the conflict between faith and doubt in a single soul, often a rabbi assumed (wrongly) to be more secure in his faith than others in the community. Very typical of the genre is "Joy" (*Gimpel the Fool*), the tale of Rabbi Bainish, who, after his third son dies, ceases to pray for his remaining three children, though all show signs of fatal illness. As the result of incessant bereavement, the rabbi succumbs to atheism, declaring that "the atheists are right. There is no justice, no Judge" (125). His atheism is not introspective, but blatant and blasphemous—"In the beginning was the dung" (126). His extremism, however, does not extend to his deeds; indeed, his practice of prayer and charity becomes more rigorous than before: "Poor men *do* exist. That's one thing of which we can be certain" (127). Singer leaves us in doubt as to whether the rabbi's continuance in good deeds is attributable to a certain afterglow of his previous lifelong piety or can be understood as the behavior of one who is naturally good, regardless of whether he believes or not. Moreover, Rabbi Bainish, like many of Singer's doubters (and, indeed, like many doubters Christian as well as Jewish since the Enlightenment), would rather know that devils and hell exist than be left with sheer emptiness. As Carlyle's Diogenes Teufelsdröckh exclaimed, in desperation, "in our age of Down-pulling and Disbelief, the very Devil has been pulled down, you cannot so much as believe in a Devil."[24]

The turning point in Rabbi Bainish's spiritual crisis comes when, during a fast, his deceased daughter appears to him in a vision and half-commands, half-implores him to rejoin the community for celebration of the new year. He does so, and in a Torah commentary delivered to the assembled guests, he reveals what he has suddenly discovered about the true relation among faith, uncertainty, and human freedom. The question at issue is why the moon is obscured at Rosh Hashanah; and the rabbi's answer is that life, for which one prays at the new year, means free choice, and freedom is predicated on mystery: "If one knew the truth how could there be freedom? If hell and paradise were in the middle of the market place, everyone would be a saint. Of all the blessings bestowed on man, the greatest lies in the fact that God's face is forever hidden from him" (131). God, the narrator implies, resides as much in darkness as in light, and He does so in order to test people. Belief is less a matter of sifting and assessing evidence than of asserting one's will.

Yet the events of the story do not harmonize with, and may even be said to belie, its assertion that true faith declares itself despite a large admixture of doubt, despite God's *hiding* his face. (In the Hebrew Bible, we recall, it is always only *something* of God that is glimpsed.) After all, what is the appearance of a dead child if not an uncovering of God's face? It is only after this miraculous appearance that the rabbi recovers the truth and his faith. He goes on to celebrate the holidays, from Rosh Hashanah through Simchas Torah (Rejoicing of the Law), with unprecedented joy, though also with a growing conviction of the unreality of the material world and the expectation of his death. Unlike most of the classical Yiddish writers, whose *this*-worldliness tends to make even religious experience subservient to social needs, Singer often grants his heroes revelation only at the price of death. Shortly after Rabbi Bainish has recovered his faith, his dead family members appear to lead him, ever so gently, into a joyous death. What begins as a story of doubt and blasphemy ends as a pastoral idyll.

Although visits from the dead occur frequently in Singer's stories about belief and doubt, they are not invariably sources of comfort to those who experience them. In "By the Light of Memorial Candles" (*Gimpel the Fool*), beggars trade tales about tantalizing hints of life from beyond the grave, of souls who have departed, yet not irrevocably. A grave digger tells of a corpse who, while he was reciting psalms over her, briefly returned to life and asked for water. From that time he could never cease to worry about burying people, including his wife, too soon. Here the incursion of death into life does nothing to strengthen faith, but instills an unnerving doubt about the fixity of boundaries between life and death (a subject also addressed in "The Man Who Came Back").

"Something Is There" (*A Friend of Kafka*) is, at least outwardly, similar to "Joy," but more subtle and complex. Here too we have a rabbi plagued by doubt, and quarreling—in a manner that is virtually traditional in Yiddish literature—with God, whom he calls to account not merely for personal afflictions but for the omnipresence of suffering and moral evil: "Jews being burned at the stake . . . yeshiva boys led to the gallows . . . violated virgins, tortured infants" (284). For the twenty-seven-year-old Rabbi Nechemia of Bechev, all problems blend into one: "Why the suffering?" The standard explanations for the existence of evil do not satisfy him: "If the Lord is omnipotent, He could reveal Himself without the aid of the Evil Host. If He is not omnipotent, then He is not really God." In his doubt and despair, Rabbi Nechemia speaks as did Rabbi Bainish and as do most of Singer's virtuous doubters: "There is neither a judge nor a judgment. All creation is a blind accident." The explicit message of "Joy," that is, that man's freedom *requires* the existence of evil as a test of free will, means nothing to Nechemia. Following the paradoxical Yiddish tradition of directly addressing the very God whose existence he has denied, Nechemia says: "You want to conceal your face? . . . So be it. You conceal your face and I will conceal mine" (286). If God does exist, it seems to be only for the purpose of bringing forth evil, endlessly requiring Abrahams to sacrifice their beloved Isaacs. Why, wonders the rabbi, should any Jew, and especially a rabbi, speak to a persecutor, pray to a torturer?

The rabbi decides to provoke God by violating the Sabbath. He defiantly lights his pipe—what better symbolic action for a new convert to Enlightenment?—and is not immediately struck down for the offense, although he feels himself "plummeting into the abyss." At first it is thrilling to be an unbeliever; with Enlightenment comes an illusion of newly acquired courage and relief, the result of freeing oneself of all yokes. But on his rail trip to Warsaw he is repelled by the coarse, brutal faces of the gentiles, in whom he sees only past and potential pogromists. These unsavory impressions further fuel his skepticism—could God have created such stench and savagery and have dispersed his chosen people among them?—but they also raise the unsettling question of what, barring his departure for another planet, the rabbi is to become once he is no longer a Jew. Could he possibly become one of these people by converting to Christianity? Again when he arrives in Warsaw, an urban hell that reeks of pitch, refuse, and smoke, one of his voices asks whether a messiah could possibly come to such a world; but a contrary voice tells him that it is precisely to counter such worldliness that piety exists.

Rabbi Nechemia finds his enlightened brother painting nude women in a dingy attic and is greeted very coolly. Here too the rabbi discovers for the first time the full range of substitute faiths that recently secularized Jews have adopted. Among the books on the floor he notices I. L. Peretz's famous story "If Not Higher," in which a secular saintliness is recommended by Peretz in the guise of Hasidic piety. He also reads a pamphlet about Zionist pioneers in Palestine, practicing yet another form of secular Jewish existence. Nechemia is unimpressed by both the Yiddishist and the Zionist attempts to perpetuate Jewish life in secular form. He says, "Such Jewishness is not for me. . . . I'd rather convert" (296). These new faiths do suggest to him that there are no "real heretics, those who believed in nothing." Men who profess atheism do seem to go on having children and even supporting wives, although "according to logic, a nonbeliever should care only for his own body and for no one else" (297). But he had not come all the way to Warsaw just to trade in one faith for another.

While in a bookstore, looking for a book called *How the Universe Came into Being*, the rabbi meets yet another advocate of secular Jewishness. For this man, enlightenment and atheism and assimilationism are themselves exploded faiths. He tells the rabbi that nothing can be known about the origins of the universe, but "we have to live without faith and without knowledge." Why, then, wonders our hero, should such a fellow as this be a Jew at all? The (uninspiring) answer he gets is that an entire people cannot be assimilated and, besides, the gentiles attack assimilated Jews quite as vehemently as they do real ones. Conversion is thus pointless. "We have to remain a people" (299), the man tells Nechemia.

Unceasingly appalled by the rottenness and cynicism of Warsaw, whose pleasures are no pleasures to him, the rabbi at last recognizes that, quite apart from questions of belief, one must choose between being Jacob or Esau: there are only two parties, and every day is election day. Disillusioned with Warsaw, with atheism, with the illogic of naturalism, Nechemia returns to Bechev. He again concludes that "there are no heretics" (310), for the whole world worships idols: people invent their own gods, then serve them. And no people does this more fervently than the Jews, the original idolators. But with this illumination the rabbi's physical strength leaves him. As in "Joy," it seems that the price of illumination is death, since it is only as he is growing numb that the rabbi asserts "something is there." Singer's affirmation of faith in such troubled rabbinic characters as Bainish and Nechemia is severely, perhaps fatally, qualified by his making it a faith that will sustain people in dying but not in living.

On the other hand, faithlessness is, in Singer's fiction, virtually a guarantee of misery and, when carried to extremes, even insanity. "The Blasphemer" (*A Friend of Kafka*) is a character sketch of a street-corner atheist named Chazkele. Like the doubting rabbis, he asks why small children die, why there are internal contradictions in the Bible and

Talmud, and so forth. But unlike the rabbis, he is also mean spirited and destructive, in a manner that Jewish secularists, unable to leave their people and religion quietly and tactfully, have often adopted. He does not merely violate all Jewish laws and norms; he shows a special ingenuity in defamation and blasphemy, as when he fastens the head phylactery (worn by Jewish males in morning prayer) between the horns of a goat and the arm phylactery to one of the animal's legs. When he does fall in love, it must be with a prostitute, whom he of course refuses to marry. He carries his atheism to its extreme form by recognizing nothing symbolic and reducing all that men and women have done over the centuries to make life human to literalness and materiality: "What is a canopy? A few yards of velvet. And what is a ketuba [marriage contract]? A piece of paper" (228). (Later incarnations of Chazkele would announce their discovery that a nation's flag was no more than a piece of cotton.) The story of this blasphemer, whose dying request is that he be cut to pieces and fed to dogs, is Singer's most direct and polemical assertion that faithlessness leads to insanity.

Jews who desert their people and religion for Christianity are often depicted by Singer as acting from some defect of character. "The Primper" (*A Friend of Kafka*) tells of an elderly spinster who all her life has been obsessed with decking herself out in the latest and best clothes and jewelry. When she is told that the splendid shrouds she has collected for her burial cannot be used because Jews are not allowed luxurious burial clothes but must all be buried alike, in simple plain linen, she decides to convert to Christianity: "The Jews shame the dead. The Christians dress a corpse in his finest. They place him in a coffin and cover him with flowers" (190). Vanity is also the reason that Zeidel Cohen, the protagonist of "Zeidlus the Pope" (*Short Friday*), converts to Christianity. This genius of the Torah, an ascetic devoted exclusively to his scholarship, is appealed to by the Evil One (the narrator of this tale) through his sole human weakness: his vanity. "It's not right that a great man such as you, a master of the Torah . . . should be buried in a God-forsaken village such as this where no one pays the slightest attention to you" (180). Satan tells Zeidel that the Christians are much more prone to make a human being into an idol than the Jews are: "Since their God is a man, a man can be a God to them" (181). Tempted by the prospect of fame, even the hope of becoming pope, Zeidel embraces Christianity and is reborn as Benedictus Janovsky. Like many actual Jewish converts, he begins to write polemical attacks against the Talmud, something he can do better than his predecessors because he actually knows something about the subject.

But soon Zeidel discovers that "even among the Gentiles things were far from perfect" (185). Instead of becoming instantly famous, he is beset by poverty and premature old age. He comes to regret his conversion, sinks into beggary, and is soon neglected by his Christian coreligionists. His Christian theology is forgotten as rapidly as he had learned it. Most important, these chastening experiences burn the vanity out of him, leaving him only with the desire to know the truth about the ultimate questions of God's existence and final judgment. Then, like many of Singer's errant Jews who find their way back to their faith and people, he simultaneously loses faith in the existence of the material world and is (too rapidly) despatched to the immaterial one.

Although most of Singer's stories about belief and disbelief center on the question of God's existence and his providential involvement in history, some serve to enforce Singer's conviction that belief of any kind, even to the point of foolish credulity, is a good in itself. They express his aggression against worldliness, which he defines in the same way Cynthia Ozick does, as the gullibility that disbelieves in everything.

"The Beggar Said So" (*The Spinoza of Market Street*) celebrates the credulity of its hero, Moshe. Solely because a beggar tells him that a chimney sweep is needed in the distant town of Yanov, Moshe responds, without further inquiry, by uprooting himself, his wife, and all his worldly goods. Upon arrival, he finds that the town already has a chimney sweep. Since he replies to all inquiries about why he made such a rash move by saying, "The beggar said so," he becomes the favorite butt of ridicule for the children of Yanov. Moshe and his wife have the necessary qualifications for Singer-bestowed sainthood: they are kind to animals, and they are incapable of righteous anger, even toward the beggar who, apparently, deceived them.

One night Moshe awakens to find that his dream about soot in the poorhouse chimney catching fire has come true. In an act of instinctive, unpremeditated heroism, Moshe puts out the fire and saves the lives of the inhabitants of the poorhouse. When investigation reveals that the incumbent chimney sweep has not done his job in months, he is dismissed and Moshe at last gets the job as Yanov's official sweep. One of the poor men he had saved turns out to be none other than the beggar who had—it is now clear—sent Moshe ahead in order to save life, just as Joseph had been sent in the Bible. Everything comes true eventually. The beggar was likely a *lamed-vovnik*, one of the thirty-six righteous men who, according to Jewish tradition, live out their days in obscurity as hidden saints, saving the world from destruction by the strength of their virtues. God will intervene in human affairs, such stories affirm, but only if people are willing to bear the brunt of ridicule in order to act upon their belief in such intervention.

In Singer's fictional world, Moshe has a famous cousin named Gimpel, the hero of his creator's best-known, most frequently anthologized, and most thoroughly studied short story (*Gimpel the Fool and Other Stories*). When Saul Bellow's translation of the story appeared in *Partisan Review* in 1953, the barrier of parochialism that once kept the American literary world ignorant of even the greatest of Yiddish writers in the United States was lowered long enough for Singer to make his escape from the cage of Yiddish into the outside world.

What mainly characterizes Gimpel is his readiness to believe everything he is told, no matter how improbable, fantastic, "incredible." He is fooled into playing truant from school by being told the lie that the rabbi's wife has been brought to childbed. When his tormentors find out how credulous he is, they give free rein to their imagination in lies: " 'Gimpel, the Czar is coming to Frampol; Gimpel, the moon fell down in Turbeen. . . .' And I like a *golem* believed everyone." He believed, he says, because traditional wisdom conveys the awareness that "everything is possible" (4).

Sometimes the tricks played on poor Gimpel touch on the most sacred things or on those by which a human being is most immediately attached to life. Told that the Messiah has come and that the dead, including his own mother and father, have arisen from the grave, Gimpel runs outside to look, even though he "knew very well that nothing of the sort had happened." Shamed by the howls of laughter that mock his apparent credulity, he momentarily resolves "to believe nothing more." But the rabbi reassures him, not—as perhaps he ought to have done—with the reminder that a believing Jew can hardly be superior and skeptical about the messianic deliverance toward which his whole religion yearns, but on moral grounds: "It is written, better to be a fool all your days than for one hour to be evil. . . . For he who causes his neighbor to feel shame loses Paradise himself."

The central foolishness of Gimpel's life is the willingness with which he allows himself to be duped (or is he?) into marrying Elka, who is (and whom Gimpel knows to be, though he is told otherwise) the town whore. She is a widow, she is divorced, and she is pregnant with a child who is born seventeen weeks after the wedding with Gimpel. Gimpel accepts the child as his own, only to be subjected to the further humiliation of finding Elka in bed with another man. At first he refuses to credit (or pretend to credit) her lies, saying that "Gimpel isn't going to be a sucker all his life. There's a limit even to the foolishness of a fool like Gimpel" (11). But two impulses keep him from asserting his dignity—and his incredulity. One is his incapacity, very like Moshe's, for righteous anger and hatred. The other is his instinctive sense that belief is not a matter of evidence but of will. This is Gimpel's positive version of that favorite negative doctrine of dogmatic thinkers, namely, that those who deny speculative truths are morally at fault and that, as the Catholic thinker John Henry Newman once wrote to a prospective convert to his faith, *"We can believe what we choose."*[25]

This link, on the surface utterly absurd, between faith in one's (unfaithful) wife and faith in God is made by Gimpel himself and does not depend on the reader's inference. "All Frampol refreshed its spirits because of my trouble and grief," says Gimpel. "However, I resolved that I would always believe what I was told. What's the good of *not* believing? Today it's your wife you don't believe; tomorrow it's God Himself you won't take stock in" (14). Gimpel never takes the analogy a step further to say that the Jewish people have been far more faithful to their God than He to them, but in the aftermath of the Holocaust there are few Jewish heads through which that thought will not at least momentarily pass when they read this passage.

Elka's continuing infidelities over two decades do try Gimpel's love and faith, but his belief in belief itself is strong enough to blot out all negative empirical evidence: "All kinds of things happened, but I neither saw nor heard. I believed, and that's all. The rabbi recently said to me, 'Belief in itself is beneficial. It is written that a good man lives by his faith' " (17). Gimpel's last temptation is proffered by Satan himself, who, after Elka's deathbed confession of her lifelong deception of Gimpel, suggests that Gimpel get even with all the inhabitants of Frampol by pouring urine in the dough of their bread. But just as Gimpel is about to risk eternal life for a dirty act of revenge, God comes to his aid by sending a message through Elka, who appears in a dream to say to Gimpel, "Because I was false is everything false too?" (19). This is God's way of keeping faith with Gimpel when his belief in his wife, the foundation on which all other beliefs have rested, crumbles. For the rest of the story, Gimpel wanders through the world as a storyteller in his own right, a sage who spins yarns about "improbable things that could never have happened" (20).

Despite Gimpel's descent from the schlemiels of the classical Yiddish writers, he differs from them in several respects. Unlike Sholom Aleichem's Kasrilevkites or Peretz's Bontsha, Gimpel *chooses* to be fooled, to be used, to forsake his dignity. This means that not only his creator but he himself is capable of irony about the sacrifices required by faith. Moreover, Gimpel's folly is connected with his credulity, whereas much of the folly of his Yiddish predecessors comes precisely from their unwillingness to credit unusual and extraordinary events, especially if those events portend evil. Thus, the crucial moment of Sholom Aleichem's "Dreyfus in Kasrilevke" comes when the lone newspaper subscriber in town reads to the citizens the news of Alfred Dreyfus's unjust conviction for treason against France. They react in violent protest, "not against the judge who had judged so badly . . . not against the generals who had sworn so falsely nor against the Frenchmen who had covered themselves with so much shame," but against Zaidle, who reads them the news. "If you stood here with one foot in heaven and one foot on earth we still wouldn't believe you. Such things cannot be! No, this cannot be! It cannot be! It cannot be!" the citizens protest. It is true that this incredulity of the Kasrilevkites is connected causally with their faith that divine truth and justice must prevail, yet it goes without saying that Gimpel in the same situation would at once have credited the grim news from France.

All this should be kept in mind when considering Ruth Wisse's suggestion that, in a sense, the most important fact about "Gimpel the Fool" is its postwar date of composition. "How," she asks, "does one retain the notion of psychic survival when its cost has been physical extinction? . . . After the entire populations of Kasrilevke and Tuneyadevke have been reduced to the ash of crematoria, does it not become a cruel sentimentality to indulge in schlemiel humor and to sustain a faith in the ironic mode?" Singer's story, she points out, is one of the rare examples in postwar Yiddish fiction of the schlemiel figure, whose development is the subject of her book. She suggests, without insisting on, the possible link between the traditional celebration of the schlemiel's innocence or gullibility and the inability or refusal of the majority of Jews "to face reality" when they were being herded into ghettos, concentration camps, and finally gas chambers.[26] She accepts the tradition (angrily repudiated by survivors like Alexander Donat) that the hymn of the camps was "Ani Maamin" ("I Believe") and implies the link with Gimpel's celebration of belief against all evidence.

But was it really their religious faith that made the majority of Jews disbelieve in the actuality of the threat that faced them? Many witnesses and survivors have alleged that, on the contrary, it was their faith in "mankind" and in the "world" that betrayed the Jews. If that is so, then we can accept "Gimpel the Fool" as a story written not in spite of, but because of, Singer's awareness of the Holocaust. If worldliness is indeed the gullibility that disbelieves everything, then this is the most intense of all Singer's assaults upon it, for Gimpel is a character who insists on believing everything. He is sternly indifferent to the voice of common sense, that faculty which, according to Hannah Arendt, was the most fatal of all to the appointed victims of the Holocaust, because it encouraged them "to explain away the intrinsically incredible by means of liberal rationalizations."[27] If, Gimpel might say, you disbelieve the nations who threaten to remove the Jewish people from the face of the earth, you will disbelieve anything.

Stories of Love, Sex, and Perversion

Rare is the Singer story that does not deal with some aspect of love. "I am," he has said, "very much interested in the relations between man and woman. This is a topic which will never be exhausted. Every man and every woman is different. And every day the same man is a different man and the same woman is a different woman. So here we have a treasure for our imagination without end."[28] He has expressed the view that we see humanity most fully through sex and love because "the sexual organs express the human soul more than any other part of the body" (Singer/Burgin, 33). If this makes Singer sound too much like some modern American novelists for whom an obsession with sex is a sign of imaginative exhaustion, a substitute for ideas and a genuine subject, we need to recall that *soul* is for Singer not an empty word, but a summoning of the moral and religious energies of human beings. As Joseph Epstein has shrewdly remarked, "I. B. Singer is . . . quite as concerned with sex as Philip Roth, but . . . with a decisive difference. In Singer's fiction, the pleasures of sex mix with terrors of guilt and sin, and somewhere off in the distance you feel perhaps God is watching. In a Roth novel, sex has to do with a writer paying respect to his 'unsocialized side,' and somewhere off in the distance you can hear a pen scratching."[29]

Although in his youth he opposed the institution of marriage altogether, Singer's own "ideal" of love is monogamy: if one god, then one wife. Yet the ideal appears far less often in his tales than the violations of it do. Indeed, to find this ideal in its pristine form one must resort (not surprisingly) to one of Singer's few short stories written in the manner of the classic Yiddish writers. "Short Friday" (*Short Friday and Other Stories*) is a pastoral, idyllic tale set in the shtetl untouched by the ravages of modernity.

The story tells of a homely, incompetent tailor and his beautiful wife, who "loved one another with a great love." They are simple people, bare of "personal" resources, material or spiritual, yet richly endowed with the wealth of a traditional religious culture that orders every detail of their lives—dressing, eating, cooking, washing, praying. Each is infinitely grateful to the other for being the vehicle of transmission of a wisdom, beauty, and piety that existed before they were born and, they believe, will continue after they die: "Here am I, a simple woman, an orphan, and yet God has chosen to bless me with a devoted husband who praises me in the holy tongue" (237). Lovemaking itself is regulated, and made human rather than animal, by religious law: "His urge was to mate with her immediately, but he remembered the law which admonished a man not to copulate with a woman until he had first spoken affectionately to her" (239). From this serene, beautiful image of harmonious love in its pre-Enlightenment form, everything else is a falling away into varieties of imperfection. In most of Singer's love stories, love is a struggle between two people; if union comes about, it is only after conflict.

Within what may be called the marriage group of Singer's tales, one may distinguish three (broadly defined) categories: stories about marriage as a completion of what is fragmentary, a fructifying of what is sterile; stories that celebrate (sometimes ambiguously) the uncanny permanence of the marriage bond; and stories that stress the spiritual limitations of marriage.

In several of Singer's stories of courtship leading toward marriage, the woman represents a creative force that can restore vitality to men in whom the springs of life have been dried up by rationalism. These women may distract men from the life of the mind and the dispassionate pursuit of truth seen under the aspect of eternity, but they supply the germinating spirit without which mind remains sterile. One of the most representative of such tales is "The Spinoza of Market Street" (*The Spinoza of Market Street*).

Spinoza, recipient of so much uncritical admiration from both Jews and gentiles during the past century and a half, is here bested not by the Judaism against which he set himself but by ignorant, untutored human love. The Spinozistic ideal of detachment from the passions, including love as well as war, is mocked by life. In the story, thirty years of devotion to Spinoza's *Ethics* have made the hero, Dr. Nahum Fischelson of Warsaw, dyspeptic and flatulent, trying without success to sustain himself on the Spinozistic doctrine that morality and happiness are identical. In his detachment, Fischelson sees two worlds: above him, in the infinite space and silence of the heavens, he glimpses "the *Amor Dei Intellectualis* which is, according to the philosopher of

Amsterdam, the highest perfection of the mind" (7); below, he sees Warsaw's Market Street, the confused multitudinousness of the world, with its thieves, prostitutes, and gamblers, "the very antithesis of reason . . . immersed in the vainest of passions" (9). Fischelson feels an un-Spinozistic anger at nearly all "modern" Jewish movements— Zionism, socialism, anarchism, postbiblical Hebrew. In his depression he even thinks of taking his own life, but then remembers that Spinoza—who does, after all, have his uses—disapproved of suicide. This rationalist is plagued by irrational dreams that persuade him of the inescapability of madness.

At this low point, Fischelson is saved by an unprepossessing spinster neighbor named Black Dobbe. This unlettered woman nurses the ailing philosopher, brings him back from the edge of death, and—without the slightest encouragement from him—arranges their marriage. Delicious stabs of satire against Spinozistic intellectualism enliven the account of this bizarre courtship. Why, she wonders, if he is a doctor, can't Fischelson write prescriptions or do much of anything to heal himself? And what, she wonders, can this beloved *Ethics* be but a gentile prayer book? So enfeebled that, at the wedding ceremony, he cannot break the glass goblet, Fischelson is certain he will not be able to consummate the marriage. But Black Dobbe's sensual determination vanquishes Spinoza and snuffs out the Enlightenment. He is saved precisely by that part of the universe which he could not light up with his intellect: "The *Ethics* dropped from his hands. The candle went out. . . . What happened that night could be called a miracle. . . . Powers long dormant awakened in him. . . . He . . . was again a man as in his youth" (22–23). Under the aspect of eternity, Dr. Fischelson's marriage in old age means little, but, the story says, people do not live entirely under the aspect of eternity; they are not rational beings, but feeling, acting, emotional ones, hence open to miraculous interference. The sterility of Jewish Enlightenment, a frequent theme of Singer's novels, is here expressed through a tale of resurrection wrought by sensuality. After consummating his marriage, Fischelson begs forgiveness: "Divine Spinoza, forgive me. I have become a fool" (24). If so, his new folly is wiser than his old wisdom.

At first, "The Shadow of a Crib" (*The Spinoza of Market Street*) appears to tell the story of a gentile Fischelson. Dr. Yaretzky, a real (i.e., medical) doctor, is a contentious materialist and atheist who frightens off matchmakers with his blasphemies: "Jesus was nothing but a lousy Jew!" (65). Yaretzky, unlike Fischelson, is a dashing, physically at-

tractive man, able (albeit unwittingly) to charm even the women he
has grossly offended into pursuing him. But he does not wish to be
caught, for he is as dedicated to Schopenhauer as Fischelson was to
Spinoza, and so holds that women are narrow-waisted, high-breasted,
wide-hipped vessels of sex trying to lure men into the swamp of marriage. When on the verge of being entrapped himself, the doctor flees.
Rejecting the joy and promise held out by marriage, "he spat at the
sky but the spittle landed on his own knee" (84). The scene suggests
that the universe itself rejects such negativism: if you adopt it, you
dirty not the universe but yourself. When Yaretzky leaves, his fiancée
becomes a nun, and dies shortly afterward of a broken heart.

So ends the earthly career of this cerebral naysayer. But fourteen
years later his ghost returns and is seen at several places in town. Some
even claim that on moonlit nights "one could see on the wall of Helena's
room, the shadow of a crib." The story complements "Spinoza," for
this doctor, unlike Fischelson, does *not* allow himself to be made a fool
by love, and so is reduced to a ghost, while his "child" remains but a
shadow. But if the story's primary message is one about unfulfillment
and sterility, mean-spirited bachelor misogyny, Singer also tantalizes
us with the suggestion that dreams of *un*realized potentialities may be
more real than the substantial, material realities that crumble to dust:
"Heaven and earth conspire that everything which has been, be rooted
out and reduced to dust. Only the dreamers, who dream while awake,
call back the shadows of the past and braid from unspun threads—
unwoven nets" (88).

In the second category of marriage stories, Singer celebrates, or at
least contemplates with awe and wonder, the durability of the conjugal
bond. In "The Unseen" (*Gimpel the Fool*) he describes a marital fidelity
that survives "ordinary" infidelity itself. The title refers to the hero,
Nathan, as he becomes after leaving his wife, Roise Temerl, whom
he has been induced to divorce by an evil spirit. After misadventures
with a devil-sent seductress, he returns, a beggar, to Roise, who by
this time has remarried. She hides him away, in a ruin, where, in
effect, she secretly (and bigamously) remarries her "unseen" original
husband. Once married, the story says, always married: "when a husband and wife sleep on one pillow they have the same head" (173).
Legal bills of divorcement mean nothing: "Can the twelve lines of a
bill of divorcement separate two souls who have been fused by fifty
years of common life?" This indissoluble bond is not kept intact by a
"sacramental" notion of marriage; after all, it is the devil himself who

urges Roise to ignore the divorce, rejoin her husband—and be damned in hell as a result. Not religion, but time and intimacy sanctify the marriage bond.

The same theme permeates "Esther Kreindel the Second" (*Short Friday*) and "Old Love" (*Passions*), though the first story is set in the European shtetl and the second in modern Miami Beach. Although Esther Kreindel is very much dead corporeally—"my body is buried under seven feet of ground, my eyes have already been consumed by the worms" (64)—her soul cannot rest, because her living husband yearns for her desperately. She therefore seeks to inhabit another body in which she may return to her husband, and finds one in a young woman named Simmele who had admired her and her wealthy family. Esther is no mere dybbuk, for Simmele actually *becomes* Esther Kreindel, taking on, in the course of time, even the physical features of the dead woman, even her habits and tics. If, in this tale, love proves strong enough to conquer death, in "Old Love" it is imperious enough to claim the living. In a pattern familiar in Singer stories, an octogenarian who has been wondering why he should continue to live is restored to new life by a widow of fifty-seven. But no sooner has this "resurrection" taken place than the widow kills herself, leaving behind this note: "Dear Harry, forgive me. I must go where my husband is. If it's not too much trouble, say Kaddish for me. I'll intercede for you where I'm going" (41). Nothing in the story indicates that she takes her life from despair, and so the narrator is left at the end to ponder the mystery of "why a man is born and why he must die" (42). The marital bond proves stronger than the bond to life itself.

Singer is also capable of less tragic formulations of the indissolubility of the marriage bond, the unity it sometimes creates between the bodies and souls of husband and wife. In "Caricature" (*The Spinoza of Market Street*), set in the Warsaw of the 1930s, Dr. Boris Margolis finds that a new generation is responding sympathetically to his work and so returns to a scholarly manuscript on which he had labored in vain for twenty-five years. But he is appalled by the mistakes, inaccuracies, and contradictions in his work, even though a willing publisher has gladly overlooked them. The more he struggles to revise this philosophical work, the more frustrated and dissatisfied he grows. His wife, who has always remained ignorant of his work, is nevertheless passionately loyal to him, defending his reputation and this book in particular at every opportunity. Dr. Margolis is even "shamed by her ignorance and her exaggerated loyalty" (106). One night he finds her, wearing his robe and slippers, seated at his desk, where she has fallen asleep in the course of reading his ailing manuscript. It dawns on him that, by dint of long proximity and intense loyalty, she has *become* her husband. "Man and wife," he thinks to himself, "share a pillow so long that their heads grow alike . . . a biological imitation" (107). But for her to become her husband is to see like her husband, and therefore, when she thinks nobody is looking, she too is disillusioned with the manuscript: "On her tightly shut lids was stamped disappointment." When she awakens, she eagerly assures him that "it's a great book, a work of genius" (108). But he knows better, and knows now that *she* knows better.

Although Judaism enjoins and sanctifies marriage, Singer is willing to acknowledge that for intensely spiritual people marriage may be a snare. The limitations of marriage, viewed from the standpoint of the spirit, are emphasized in "The Riddle" and "Altele" (*A Friend of Kafka*). In the first story, a saintly, ascetic, puny Oyzer-Dovidl is oddly matched with a sensual, flirtatious wife, Nechele, whose marital dissatisfaction is a "riddle" to her husband, though not to anyone else. He pities gentiles as eaters of swine's flesh who rejected the Torah when the Lord offered it to them and who have dwelt in spiritual darkness ever since. But while he yearns for the end of the exile, his wife yearns for flesh, and not merely gentile flesh but the flesh of the son of the local pork butcher, with whom she runs off on the eve of Yom Kippur, the holiest time of the Jewish liturgical year. The story's ending is equally compounded of Oyzer-Dovidl's humiliation and joy: "One of his eyes seems to weep, the other to laugh. After these evil tidings the way to saintliness lay open before him. All temptations were gone. Nothing was left but to love God and to serve him until the last breath." The story thus turns, surprisingly, into one of the strongest affirmations in Singer of the view he often attributes to his rigid, reactionary father, that the world itself is *treyf* (unclean).[30] The hero's suspicion that sensuality, gentiles, animality, and worldliness are all one is confirmed by his wife's obscene, blasphemous betrayal, which humiliates him in the eyes of others but also frees him to pursue righteousness.

"Altele" is a complement to "The Riddle," and appears directly after it in the collection entitled *A Friend of Kafka*. Altele, beautiful and so intensely devout that she "prayed three times daily, avoided looking at men, and even kept her eyes away from dogs and pigs," marries a devout teacher's assistant named Grunam Motl. But the marriage is barren, despite Altele's willingness to try, year after year, even the most superstitious remedies, "anything to bring a child into the world." She is abandoned by her husband, whom she rediscovers in a poorhouse after five years of searching for him. Although they are formally reunited by a rabbi, Grunam Motl is no longer interested in sleeping with her. Reverting willingly now to the role of abandoned wife, she leaves her "real" husband and sets out once more "to look for her lost husband." As in the case of Oyzer-Dovidl in "The Riddle," Altele's misfortune, as it seems to the members of the community, opens the way to awareness of a spiritual realm beyond the fleshly bond between husband and wife. Altele believes that her literal abandonment by Grunam Motl was only an extreme version of every wife's lot in marriage: "True love between man and wife begins only in Paradise, where the man sits on a golden chair and his wife serves as his footstool, and both are initiated into the mysteries of the Torah. Here on earth . . . a woman is an abandoned wife even when she rests her head next to her husband's on the same pillow." Like Oyzer-Dovidl, she finds that deprivation of worldly satisfaction can open the way to awareness of a craving for nourishment that comes only from the spiritual world; but since she is a woman, her craving is itself defined as a search for a celestial husband rather than for God.

For many, Singer is well aware, marriage is tedious, and so they explore the rich possibilities of excitement and "individuation" offered by wickedness in its infinite varieties. In "The Mirror" (*Gimpel the Fool*) the heroine, Zirel, is enticed by the devil-narrator into a mirror and whisked off to Sodom. Beautiful and well educated, she suffers from the fatal modern disease of boredom in her little Polish shtetl, and so is taken by the demon to the more exciting town of Sodom, where there's plenty of action, especially sexual. There various devils contend for her favors, tearing at her until she begs for pity; but there is no salvation, or even relief, for her. Singer has himself said of the story, "The idea is more or less that we run away from boredom into wickedness and there is almost nothing between." Wickedness too can become boring, however, since the demon "has so much perversion around him that he's yearning for some natural love" (Singer/Howe, 33).

Sexuality, like all things originally good (and perhaps more than most), is liable to perversion if carried to excess. Nowhere in Singer's fiction is the perversion to which sexuality is liable, and the grotesque forms of which all life is capable, expressed with more force than in the story "Blood" (*Short Friday*). Although, as Singer is fond of remarking, the cabalists attributed sex even to God, they also knew that "the passion for blood and the passion for flesh have the same origin, and this is the reason 'Thou shalt not kill' is followed by 'Thou shalt not commit adultery.' " The story "Blood" strictly illustrates, in the career of its main character, Risha, the truth of this ancient dictum.

The twice-widowed Risha has married the pious and (as his surname denotes) honest Reb Falik Erlichman, a man thirty years her senior. Although endowed with the high bosom and "broad hips" of Schopenhauer's insatiable life force, she has never borne a child, and she never will. As her husband departs from active life into piety and old age, Risha becomes enamored of Reuben the butcher, precisely because of his prowess at slaughtering animals. Reuben, though coarse, fleshy, and lecherous, is linked, as a ritual slaughterer, with religion itself. He reminds Risha of this fact in his rejection of her (pretended) pity for his victims: "When you scale a fish on the Sabbath, do you think the fish enjoys it?" (30). Within the confines of piety itself, Singer mischievously intimates, there is compulsory cruelty, a point made much more insistently in the zealously vegetarian story "The Slaughterer" (*The Séance*), whose hero "could not bear the sight of blood."

Risha discovers that her lust is aroused by watching Reuben slaughter hens and roosters. At first she wishes to identify with his victims by copulating with him: "In their amorous play, she asked him to slaughter her. Taking her head, he bent it back and fiddled with his finger across her throat. When Risha finally arose, she said to Reuben: 'You certainly murdered me that time' " (33). As Risha reduces herself more and more to the state of the human animal, the old figure of the "beast with two backs" is literally realized, and the panting of the lovers is provoked by and indistinguishable from the death rattles of the animals in whose straw they rustle.

Having begun by identifying with the victim, Risha goes a step further and identifies with the slaughterer himself. Although she has studied neither the *Shulchan Aruch* nor the Commentaries that a slaughterer is required to know, she insists on taking over Reuben's work. As Irving Buchen points out,[31] this usurpation of the male role is a crucial element in the growth of Risha's perversion. But its ultimate significance lies in the fact that if you live for pleasure, you must aspire to the ultimate pleasure of murder itself. Risha becomes dominant even over the brutal Reuben because her killing is done solely for pleasure and cannot be confined within the bounds of ritual.

Despite Reuben's protests, therefore, Risha not only slaughters animals but practices deception upon the Jewish community by slaughtering horses and pigs and selling them as kosher beef. This action gives her a pleasure on a par with lechery and cruelty, and demonstrates that any single sin both invites and encompasses all others. Sexuality, Singer shows, is not something universally to be encouraged, for among the wicked it is essentially violent.

Eventually, Risha and Reuben are discovered. Set upon by a mob, Reuben flees and Risha becomes a convert to Christianity. By this device she not only affords herself protection but joins those who command the weapons of slaughter and separates herself from the eternally victimized Jews. But once her husband drops dead of shock, she can no longer derive any pleasure from lust and slaughter, for there is no one for her to betray and mock. Tormented in dreams by the phantoms of animals, Risha turns into a carnivorous beast, a ravening werewolf, and is at last fatally wounded by the Jews of Laskev. Despite a life of sexual abandon, despite her three husbands and her gargantuan sexual exploits with the lascivious butcher—now turned vegetarian penitent—Risha has produced nothing. It is as if the energy that in a normal woman goes into procreation cannot be inert but must, if not expended in the creation of life, work toward its destruction.

But what is a "normal" woman? Does one dare, in the midst of so much contemporary noise on this subject, suggest that biology partly determines the answer? If "Blood" approaches an answer by analyzing the perversion of sexual passion, "Yentl the Yeshiva Boy" (*Short Friday*) is one of Singer's most balanced, tactful, and restrained treatments of the subject of the perversion to which even the noblest of human impulses—the disinterested passion for wisdom and love—may lead. Yentl's troubles had begun when her bedridden father studied the Torah with her just as if she were a boy, and she proved so apt a pupil that her whole soul yearned toward the world of Torah scholarship. But that very world had itself decreed that only men's souls could yearn toward such a consummation, whereas women were to fulfill themselves in the production and rearing of Jewish children. What reader of Yiddish literature can forget the satirical thrust of the question put by Miriam, the heroine of Peretz's "Devotion without End," to the angels of paradise who, believing her to be a man (the husband for whom she sacrificed herself), ask her whether she studied the Torah: "She smiled charmingly: 'Lord of the Universe, have you ever directed the daughters of Israel to study your Torah?' "

"Yentl" is the kind of story that can easily be misconstrued by readers unfamiliar with Jewish life and that will almost certainly be misconstrued by readers of the feminist persuasion. Although Yentl is in many respects, including the physical, "not cut out for a woman's life," it is explicitly her desire to study the Torah that propels her into the drastic decision to dress herself as a man and enter a yeshiva. For feminism, as for all the varied offspring of leftist ideology, Singer has nothing but contempt. But Yentl is treated with sympathy (partial, to be sure) because she wants equality not as a woman with men but as a Jew with other Jews.

Singer's resistance toward Yentl's ambition arises from two sources. One is his traditionalist view that Judaism depends on distinction and separation: weekday from Sabbath, gentile from Jew, meat from milk, woman from man. Therefore the story frequently endorses the wisdom of the commandment that "a woman shall not wear that which pertaineth to a man." Singer believes that far more than a sartorial preference underlies this prohibition, for Yentl's blurring of the distinction between the sexes deceives both herself and others, perverts her life, and harms everyone associated with her. Primary among her unintended victims are Avigdor, her yeshiva study partner and soul brother, and Hadass, whom Yentl (or Anshel, the man's name she adopts) actually marries.

Although Yentl-Anshel marries Hadass for the highest of motives— to recover her for Avigdor, whose fiancée Hadass had been—she thereby entangles herself in sin and depravity. Hadass, to be sure, loves her Anshel and is so innocent that she doesn't know (and doesn't care) that she is not truly married. They are tender and loving to each other. Yet Singer never allows us to forget that whatever else may be said for homosexual relationships, they do not do much for the propagation of the race and perpetuation of the Jewish people. This is Singer's second, insuperable objection to Yentl's ambition to dedicate her life to the study of the Torah.

Yet Singer does not entirely withdraw his sympathy from Yentl. Even after she reveals her true identity to Avigdor, they continue to study the Torah together, a scholarly David and Jonathan: "Though their bodies were different, their souls were of one kind." This being so, Yentl is quite right to reply to Avigdor's desperate suggestion that they both seek divorces in order to marry each other that "I wanted to study the Gemara and Commentaries with you, not darn your socks" (154– 55).

The story's practical problem is resolved by the disappearance of Yentl and the marriage of Hadass (to whom Yentl sends divorce papers) to Avigdor. The true purpose of marriage, thwarted by homosexuality, is now fulfilled: "Not long after the wedding, Hadass became pregnant" (159). But gain must be measured against loss. What has been lost is the Torah scholar named Yentl, who by symbolic extension stands for whole generations of potential Torah scholars lost to the Jewish people through an accident of birth.[32]

Vegetarian Tales

In *The Estate*,[33] a continuation of *The Manor*, a character named Zadok, the wayward son of a Hasid, expounds the view that history and nature use humankind merely as raw material for the fulfillment of their superhuman purposes. Zadok believes, in the manner of "social Darwinians," that the moral laws of the Jews are confuted by the laws of biology that sanction and even require the Malthusian struggle for existence and catastrophic wars: "It's the same to nature who kills whom. For thousands of years bulls have been slaughtered and nature has kept quiet. . . . Why should a human life be so dear to Nature?"

Zadok's allusion to the slaughter of bulls as a model for the slaughter of people serves to remind us that Singer's vegetarianism, however embarrassing it has been to many of his admirers, is crucial to his understanding of the evil deeply embedded in history and in nature itself. "I am a sincere vegetarian," Singer has said, adding:

> Even though I don't have any dogma, this has become my dogma. I have convinced myself that as long as we are going to be cruel to animals, as long as we are going to apply towards animals the principle that might makes right, I think that the Higher Powers will apply the same principle to us. They are mightier than we are, and to whom, perhaps, we are as little intelligent as the animals are in proportion to us. This is lately my kind of religion, and I really hope that one day humanity will make an end to this eating of meat and hunting of animals for pleasure.[34]

Given the historic vulnerability of the Jews, Singer's conviction that acceptance in any form of the theory that might makes right must eventually victimize the Jews explains his frequent—and apparently licentious—transfer of Holocaust language to remarks about the miserable destiny of most animals. For Herman Broder, the hero of the novel *Enemies*,[35] what the Nazis had done to the Jews, man was doing to animals. Singer's saints, like Jochanan in *The Manor*, are not merely troubled by the slaughter of animals for food but express tenderness over flies and bugs, as if they could sense that it was to be a short step from the metaphorical depiction of Jews as parasites to their literal "extermination" as bedbugs.

Singer has told how he came gradually to the belief that vegetarianism was a necessary condition of throwing back the tide of blood that flowed over the course of history, and especially of Jewish history. (It could never be a *sufficient* condition of messianic gentleness between lion and lamb. Hitler was a vegetarian, and his adhesion to Singer's "dogma" does not seem to have allayed his appetite for blood.) Singer insists:

> You cannot be gentle while you're killing a creature, you cannot be for justice while you take a creature which is weaker than you and slaughter it, and torture it. I've had this feeling since I was a child. . . . But somehow my parents told me that this means that I am trying to have more compassion than the Almighty. . . . But at another stage of my life, about twenty years ago [about 1963], I felt that I would be a real hypocrite if I would write or speak against bloodshed while I would be shedding blood myself. There's nothing profound about it, it's just an emotion. (Singer/Burgin, 152)

Ritual slaughterers play an important role in Singer's fiction, just as they did in the Jewish world of Eastern Europe that is his usual subject. The narrator of "Guests on a Winter Night" (*A Friend of Kafka*) alludes to a folk belief that "all slaughterers were born under the sign of Mars and if they had not studied to become slaughterers they would have been murderers" (18). We have already seen how, in "Blood" (*Short Friday*), a lascivious woman finds that nothing arouses her promiscuous lust more than watching a ritual slaughterer go about his daily, bloody tasks. But when the lovers' potent mixture of lechery, cruelty, and animal slaughter brings disaster, the slaughterer—Reuben—seeks penitence in a way peculiarly suited to his past: "Reuben the slaughterer . . . wandered from town to town, eating no meat, fasting Mondays and Thursdays . . . repenting his abominations" (46).

If the vegetarian impulse is important in "Blood," it is all-pervasive in the powerful and ambitious story "The Slaughterer" (*The Séance*). Its hero, Yoineh Meir, frustrated in his ambition to become the Kolomir rabbi, instead accepts the post of the town's ritual slaughterer. He does so reluctantly, however, because he is softhearted and cannot bear the sight of blood. Like the young Singer, he is admonished that "man may not be more compassionate than the Almighty, the Source of all compassion" (18). But neither argument nor invocation of biblical authority and precedent can assuage his horror of what he is doing: "The killing of every beast, great or small, caused him as much pain as though he were cutting his own throat. Of all the punishments that could have been visited upon him, slaughtering was the worst" (19–20).

Paradoxically, the more that his profession stinks in his nostrils, the greater is his revulsion from all things material, not only the stomachs, intestines, hearts, lungs, and livers that constantly surround him but even his own body. One extreme drives its practitioner to yearn toward its opposite, for he now sees all human beings under the aspect of animals destined for slaughter and the ensuing fleshly corruption: "Every neck reminded Yoineh Meir of the knife. Human beings, like beasts, had loins, veins, guts, buttocks. One slash of the knife and those solid householders would drop like oxen" (21).

The slaughterer's profession also gives him a new awareness of how intricately involved is life itself—never mind the *eating* of animals—with the use of slaughtered animals: "All his life he had slept on a feather bed, under a feather quilt, resting his head on a pillow; now he was suddenly aware that he was lying on feathers and down plucked from fowl" (22). This shock of recognition might well turn a man away from vegetarianism in the direction of an understanding that all existence is "wrong" and that simply to be alive is to be a killer. The American novelist John Updike likes to make this point by noting that the Indian sect called the Jains, who believe that everything in the universe, even matter, is eternal, wear gauze masks to avoid inhaling insects.[36] But Singer, far from accepting this reductio ad absurdum as an invalidation of vegetarianism, uses it as a powerful confirmation.

Yoineh Meir's overwhelming sense of himself as a fleshly prison within which a soul has incongruously been locked threatens to stifle him: "Father in heaven, I cannot breathe" (23). His anguish is greatest during Elul, the month of repentance for Jews. The ritual of offering a sacrificial fowl before the Day of Atonement, the holiest day in the Jewish calendar, reminds him with fresh immediacy that "each holiday brings its own slaughter. Millions of fowl and cattle now alive were doomed to be killed" (24).

At this point in the story, the reader may sense (without being at all sure that Singer does) a rift between Singer the vegetarian-reformer and Singer the artist. If Yoineh Meir's preternatural sensitivity to the plight of animals qualifies him as a potential Singer saint, it also disqualifies him for living in this world. George Eliot, in *Middlemarch*, wrote that "if we had a keen vision and feeling of all ordinary human life, it would be like hearing the grass grow and the squirrel's heart beat, and we should die of that roar which lies on the other side of silence. As it is, the quickest of us walk about well wadded with stupidity."[37]

Yoineh Meir, stripped bare of all "natural" stupidity and insensibility, is beset by nightmares in which "cows assumed human shape, with beards and side locks, and skullcaps over their horns. Yoineh Meir would be slaughtering a calf, but it would turn into a girl. . . . He even dreamed that he had slaughtered Reitze Doshe [his wife] instead of a sheep" (24).

In Jewish religious life there is an intimate connection between the killing of animals and the celebration of holidays, often if only because a great feast is at the center of the celebration. Sholem Aleichem exploited this connection brilliantly in his allegorical tale "The Pair," set during the holiday of Passover, festival of freedom. He wrote of the imprisonment, "persecution," and eventual slaughter of two roosters in a stark, horrifying way that brought him closer to the brutal violence of the pogrom than he usually came in his tales of human beings. Singer, in "Cockadoodledoo" (*The Séance*), uses a rooster-narrator whose main uncertainty is about whether he will be killed on Yom Kippur, Passover, or Succoth. He begs his audience to "listen sometimes to the roosters crowing the night before Yom Kippur when you people are reciting the midnight prayers. If your human ears could hear our weeping, you would throw away all your slaughtering knives" (81). Yoineh Meir, the slaughterer, having heard this weeping, becomes rebellious and blasphemous. Why, he asks, mourn the destruction of the Temple when he himself is Titus and Nebuchadnezzar to the animals? He is revolted by the phylacteries that are part of the daily morning prayer ritual because the parchment in them comes from the hide of a cow, and the cases of the phylacteries are made of calf's leather: "Father in Heaven. Thou art a slaughterer!" (29).

Singer the vegetarian-reformer endows Yoineh Meir with his own reverence and love for the uniqueness of being, the special "claims" of all creation: "An unfamiliar love welled up in Yoineh Meir for all that crawls and flies, breeds and swarms. Even the mice—" (26). But Singer the artist remains faithful to the truth of character and his sense of how the world works. The more diligently Yoineh Meir seeks the divine spark in mice and worms, the more fatally divorced does he become from the natural as well as the supernatural realm. The very animals whose nature he comes to respect as sacred are not notable for their respect for the sanctity of all life. The cats, for example, do not share Yoineh Meir's reluctance to kill mice.

Vegetarianism carried to its extreme, radical form alienates the slaughterer from nature and religion, and brings him to the conviction, so long resisted, that he is indeed more compassionate than God Almighty. From blasphemy it is a short step to madness, and from madness to suicide. The spectacularly lurid final vision of the story shows Yoineh Meir in flight from "myriads of cows and fowls . . . ready to take revenge for every cut, every wound, every slit gullet, every plucked feather. With bleeding throats, they all chanted, 'Everyone may kill, and every killing is permitted' " (30). Cursing God as a murderer, Yoineh Meir drowns himself.

At his best, Singer uses the vegetarian theme to reveal the profound injustice at the heart of the universe. Sometimes a sharp image, as of the dead or dying fish in "Alone" (*Short Friday*), will do this as well as an entire narrative: "We rode past a pier where freshly caught fish were being weighed. Their bizarre colors, gory skin wounds, glassy eyes, mouths full of congealed blood, sharp-pointed teeth—all were evidence of a wickedness as deep as the abyss. Men gutted the fishes with an unholy joy" (53). In "The Fast" (*Short Friday*), it requires but a single glimpse of an ox being slaughtered by a butcher to drive the main character not only into revulsion from meat but into abstinence from milk, eggs, bread, potatoes, greens—and carnal relations—for what man's killing of animals here symbolizes is the incommensurability between moral principles and human existence itself. Perhaps that is why Singer's vegetarian heroes, like his religious mystics, can usually resolve their quandaries only in the next world.

Holocaust Stories

Although the Holocaust appears at the edge or below the surface of countless of Singer's stories, it is rarely their main subject and rarely approached directly. For the most part, Singer observes that principle of literary tact which states that there is something suspect in any imaginative literary representation of the unimaginable and unprecedented atrocities of the Holocaust, whether of the outdoor killing operations in Russia or the death factories producing thousands of corpses a day in such abattoirs as Auschwitz, Maidanek, Treblinka, and Chelmno. Singer's fellow Yiddish writer, Aaron Zeitlin, expressed this principle as follows: "Were Jeremiah to sit by the ashes of Israel today, he would not cry out a lamentation, nor would he drown the desolate places with his tears. The Almighty Himself would be powerless to open up his well of tears. He would maintain a deep silence. For even an outcry is now a lie, even tears are mere literature, even prayers are false."[38]

Singer's relative reticence in dealing with this subject derives also from his feeling that this particular historical event cannot be encompassed by his usual theological assurance that there are no gaps in the cosmic order and that a providential scheme exists even though we may not discern its workings. In an autobiographical tale called "The Son" (*A Friend of Kafka*), which recounts the author's meeting with an Israeli son he had not seen in twenty years, the narrator describes a Lithuanian rabbi preaching to the disciples who have come to greet him: "I heard him say, Torah . . . Torah. . . . I wanted to ask him why the Torah hadn't defended those millions of Jews and kept them from Hitler's crematoria. But why ask him when I knew the answer already?—'My thoughts are not your thoughts.' To be martyred in God's name is the highest privilege" (249). This outburst is a rough digression from the main business of the story, yet hardly is Singer back on the narrative track when he returns to his digression as if with the feeling that more is wanted than the angry blasphemy he often assigns to his characters; and the "more" consists of an acknowledgment that the incommensurability between divine and human comprehension of the Holocaust is absolute and intolerable. The narrator continues: "Somewhere in the ditches of Poland are the ashes of those who were burned. In Germany, the former Nazis lie in their beds, each one with his list of murders, tortures . . . rapes. Somewhere there must be a Knower who knows every thought of each human being. . . . I spoke to him. Well, Almighty Knower, for you everything is just. You know the whole and have all the information . . . and that's why you're so clever. But what shall I do with my crumbs of facts?" (249–50).

These crumbs are scattered through Singer's stories that use, even though they are rarely "about," the Holocaust. It generally appears in the memories (whether actual or hallucinated) of survivors, through the mordant reflections of those who have lost their families in the European catastrophe, or through the attempt of a narrator (a thinly disguised Singer) to define his relation to the buried life of European Jewry. These stories cannot be understood without some awareness that their author, although he has lived in America for more than a half-century, has never left Poland. It is not only, as Irving Howe has said, that Singer continues to write about Polish-Jewish communities such as Lublin, Bilgoray, and Kreshev as if they still existed, but that a Poland that no longer exists is more real to him than the American cities, such as New York or Miami, where he lives.[39]

We see this very clearly in "The Lecture" (*The Seance*), one of many first-person narratives growing out of Singer's adventures and misadventures on the lecture circuit. Singer has lectured so widely (probably in every American state as well as Canada, Latin America, and Israel) that his stories about occurrences on his lecture tours constitute a subgroup in themselves. This story is told by a famous Yiddish writer called N. who has traveled by train from New York to Montreal in order to deliver what must have been an intriguing lecture, for it is "an optimistic report on the future of the Yiddish language" (65). But we never learn more of the lecture than that it "predicted a brilliant future for Yiddish" (66), because a snowstorm slows the train and makes the writer late for his appearance. In any case, he later loses the manuscript, a mishap that does not entirely displease him, because it means that "people will hear fewer lies" (70) and that he will not have to bear the burden of explaining how it is that Yiddish can have a bright future when all empirical evidence suggests its imminent demise.

In "The Lecture" the author indulges in a wry and ironic depreciation of himself in his character as a writer in a dead, or at least a dying, language. But the center of the story is more somber still, for what it says about the Yiddish writer is that everything draws him back to the subject of the Holocaust, and that for him artistic detachment is therefore an impossibility. The problem of the Yiddish writer is not only the future, but the past. The only two members of the Montreal Jewish society willing to brave the storm in order to collect Mr. N. at the station at two-thirty in the morning are a loquacious survivor of the death camps and her daughter. So lame that she can barely walk, the older woman has risked her life in order to welcome her favorite writer, whose stories had lifted some of the darkness from her heart when she first read them in the DP (displaced persons) camps after the war. After such a tribute, and in view of the lateness of the hour, Mr. N. can hardly refuse the invitation to spend the night at the apartment of these two women.

He quickly discovers that it is only physically that this old, crippled woman lives in Montreal. Her mental life is among the murdered, who include her three sons. In fact, she has even carried her old ambience to the new world. The street where she lives reminds Mr. N. of a small town in Poland—murky, narrow, lined with wooden houses. The apartment is shabby, icy, and filled with the smells of that dead world: "In some mysterious way the mother and daughter had managed to bring with them the whole atmosphere of wretched poverty from their old home in Poland" (74). It is precisely at the point he has assimilated all this that the writer discovers the loss of his manuscript. He aptly describes it as a "Freudian" accident, for it pointedly tells him that Yiddish is now irrevocably bound not merely to the Jewish past but to the destroyed world of East European Jewry. Yiddish literature is kept from artistic freedom, or perhaps saved from artistic irresponsibility, by the immediacy of the Yiddish writer's involvement with the uniquely terrible fate of modern Jewry. Giving up his manuscript for lost, Mr. N., suffering from the iciness of his room, tries by an act of imaginative sympathy to place himself in the Holocaust world of his two hostesses: "Let me imagine that I had remained under Hitler in wartime. Let me get some taste of that, too. . . . I imagined myself somewhere in Treblinka or Maidanek. I had done hard labor all day long. . . . Tomorrow there would probably be a 'selection,' and since I was no longer well, I would be sent to the ovens" (77). Mr. N. now sounds much like the Singer who prefaces *Enemies* with the curious remark that "I did not have the privilege of going through the Hitler holocaust."

Few readers will fail to sense something meretricious in this "sympathetic" identification, facile and unearned, with the victims of the Holocaust. Indeed, Singer's own uneasiness about it is suggested by the fact that while Mr. N. indulges himself in vicarious suffering and death, the real survivor, the elderly woman a few feet away from him, dies as a result of the strain of having gone to welcome him in subfreezing weather. Thus Mr. N., just an instant after imagining himself as one of Hitler's victims, finds himself sharing responsibility with Hitler for the death of a Jewish woman. Left alone with the corpse, he is swept away by the pull of wretchedness and tragedy to the old life in Poland. So insubstantial do his many years in New York now seem that he checks his citizenship papers to assure himself that "my years in America had not been an invention" (78). The Yiddish writer who writes about Jewish Poland as if it still existed cannot help returning to the Holocaust, which put an end to Jewish Poland. Yet the question of whether the search for imaginative identification with the victims can have any productive result besides "mere literature" remains unanswered.

Two stories set in modern Manhattan illustrate the way in which the Holocaust has so deeply penetrated Jewish consciousness that both its criminals and their victims lurk just beneath the surface of everyday life. The protagonist of "The Letter Writer" (*The Seance*), Herman Gombiner, having lost all his family in the Holocaust, now seeks fellowship in writing letters to total strangers. But his true communion is with the dead, more real to him than the inhabitants of Manhattan: "He sat praying for them to appear to him. The spirit cannot be burned, gassed, hanged, shot. Six million souls must exist somewhere" (262–63).

In a daydream induced by illness, Gombiner's prayer appears to be answered, for he finds himself back in the old country among his murdered relatives, and "they were all living." But as he descends farther in imagination toward Canal Street in lower Manhattan he finds himself in a tunnel that leads to a charnel house "full of the bones of corpses, slimy with decay," supervised by a grave digger. " 'How can anyone live here?' Herman asked himself. 'Who would want such a livelihood?' " The answer is, Singer, in whose work the Jews of Eastern Europe are "all living," just as if their world had not abruptly ended in death and ashes and smoke. Thus the dreamlike descent from modern Manhattan into a subterranean cemetery becomes a parable of Singer's daring imaginative enterprise as a writer of fiction.

"The Cafeteria" (*A Friend of Kafka*) recounts several meetings between the narrator, a successful Yiddish writer named Aaron, and a father and daughter who had survived both Russian and German camps during the war. Neither survived intact, for the father lost his legs, the daughter her husband and her innocence. Both have become cynical about love as a result of the animal promiscuity they claim to have observed in the camps. Even more than is usually the case in such stories, Singer calls attention to his authorial presence in the figure of the narrator, who complains, for example, that the *cafeterianiks* "reproached me for all kinds of literary errors; I contradicted myself, went too far in descriptions of sex, described Jews in such a way that anti-Semites could use it for propaganda" (85).

Although Aaron is so prosperous a writer that most of his earnings are taxed away from him, he is irresistibly drawn to the café on upper Broadway by his appetite for incessant discussion of Yiddish literature, the Holocaust, and Israel—and for Esther, who (like the women in "The Lecture" and indeed most literate women in Singer's stories) has conceived an idolatrous devotion for the hero's writing. One night the café mysteriously burns down; and four years after the event Aaron hears Esther's "explanation" of why it had to be destroyed. Shortly before the conflagration Esther had passed the cafeteria at two or three in the morning and, noticing a glow inside, entered to discover a group of men dressed in white robes, "like doctors or orderlies, all with swastikas on their sleeves," speaking German, and riveted to a speech being delivered by Hitler in "that abominable voice" familiar to her from European radio broadcasts. She fled when the men saw her, and when she returned later in the morning, the cafeteria had burned down. "Those who were there wanted all traces erased" (90–91). Aaron, at first skeptical about her tale, later concludes that "if time and space are nothing more than forms of perception . . . why shouldn't Hitler confer with his Nazis in a cafeteria on Broadway. Esther . . . had caught a glimpse behind the curtain of the phenomena." But if glimpses behind the curtain to the ultimate truths so often reveal Hitler or his victims, then the author would seem to be admitting the permanent imprint of that catastrophe. Is this not, after all, what was meant by the phrase *crime against humanity*, that is to say, the permanent alteration of the universe through the removal of one member of the family of nations?

Perhaps it is a reflection on the inability of American Jewish life to create a culture and an inner world of its own that Singer's American characters, especially the survivors, are so easily ripped out of the present by memory of the Holocaust. Although "A Wedding in Browns-ville" (*Short Friday*) shows very little interest in American Jewish so-ciology, it starts from the observation that "American Judaism was a mess" (191). This is the view of the tale's protagonist, Dr. Margolin, all of whose faith in humanity has been destroyed, along with his family, in the Holocaust. His faith in God has fared no better, for he has never been able to understand why God needed to create a Hitler or Stalin to carry out his will.

Even upon so joyous an occasion as a wedding, the black shadow of the Holocaust descends. Half the people Margolin inquires about were murdered: "He heard the same words over and over again: died, shot, burned" (200). One man insists that, in fact, all Jews are really dead because "even the survivors carry death in their hearts." Then, as if to confirm his words, something happens that makes Margolin think he may be dead himself, killed in an automobile accident he was involved in en route to the wedding. How else to explain the sudden appearance at the wedding of Raizel, the great love of his youth, long believed to have been shot by the Nazis? Or has the Messiah come, and raised the dead to life? The story ends with the hero and his ambiguously resurrected love hovering between past and present, life and death. An eerie, tantalizing, unresolved story, "A Wedding in Brownsville" expresses the author's powerful yearning to break through the boundaries that separate life and death, and dream into existence the world that was erased by the Holocaust.

Notes to Part 1

1. *The Séance and Other Stories* (New York: Farrar, Straus & Giroux, 1968). Page references to stories in this volume are given parenthetically in the text.

2. *A Friend of Kafka and Other Stories* (New York: Farrar, Straus & Giroux, 1970). Page references to stories in this volume are given parenthetically in the text.

3. *A Crown of Feathers and Other Stories* (New York: Farrar, Straus & Giroux, 1973). Page references to stories in this volume are given parenthetically in the text.

4. David Neal Miller, *Fear of Fiction: Narrative Strategies in the Works of Isaac Bashevis Singer* (Albany: State University of New York Press, 1985).

5. Joel Blocker and Richard Elman, "An Interview with Isaac Bashevis Singer," *Commentary* 36 (November 1963): 368. Subsequent references to this interview, abbreviated as Blocker/Elman, will be given parenthetically in the text.

6. *Passions and Other Stories* (New York: Farrar, Straus & Giroux, 1975). Page references to stories in this volume are given parenthetically in the text.

7. *The Family Moskat* (New York: Alfred A. Knopf, 1950).

8. *The Manor* (New York: Farrar, Straus & Giroux, 1967).

9. "Problems of Yiddish Prose in America," *Prooftexts* 9 (1989): 5–12. (Translated from the Yiddish by Robert H. Wolf.)

10. *Short Friday and Other Stories* (New York: Farrar, Straus & Giroux, 1964). Page references to stories in this volume are given parenthetically in the text.

11. *The Spinoza of Market Street and Other Stories* (New York: Farrar, Straus & Giroux, 1961). Page references to stories in this volume are given parenthetically in the text.

12. Isaac Bashevis Singer and Richard Burgin, *Conversations with Isaac Bashevis Singer* (Garden City, N.Y.: Doubleday, 1985), 89–90. Subsequent references to this book, identified as Singer/Burgin, are given parenthetically in the text.

13. Maurice Samuel, *In Praise of Yiddish* (New York: Cowles, 1971), 7.

14. "The Shtetl World," *Kenyon Review* 24 (Winter 1962): 173–77.

15. Yosef Hayim Yerushalmi, *Zakhor: Jewish History and Jewish Memory* (Seattle: University of Washington Press, 1982), 9–10.

16. *Gimpel the Fool and Other Stories* (New York: Noonday Press, 1957). Page references to stories in this volume are given parenthetically in the text.

17. Introduction to *A Treasury of Yiddish Stories* (New York: Viking, 1953), 86.

18. "Israel the Ever-Dying People," in *Modern Jewish Thought*, ed. Nahum N. Glatzer (New York: Schocken Books, 1977), 140.

19. *Satan in Goray* (New York: Noonday Press, 1955).

20. Isaac Bashevis Singer and Irving Howe, "Yiddish Tradition vs. Jewish Tradition: A Dialogue," *Midstream* 19 (June/July 1973): 36. Subsequent references to this article, identified as Singer/Howe, are given parenthetically in the text.

21. See, on this subject, Edward Alexander, "The Incredibility of the Holocaust," in *The Resonance of Dust: Essays on Holocaust Literature and Jewish Fate* (Columbus: Ohio State University Press, 1979).

22. "Dr. Fischelson's Miracle: Duality and Vision in Singer's Fiction," in *The Achievement of Isaac Bashevis Singer*, ed. Marcia Allentuck (Carbondale: Southern Illinois University Press, 1969).

23. *The Image and Other Stories* (New York: Farrar, Straus & Giroux, 1985). Page references to stories in this volume are given parenthetically in the text.

24. "The Everlasting No," *Sartor Resartus* (1831).

25. *Letters and Diaries of John Henry Newman*, ed. C. S. Dessain (Oxford: Clarendon, 1978), 12:228.

26. Ruth R. Wisse, *The Schlemiel as Modern Hero* (Chicago: University of Chicago Press, 1971), 60–67.

27. *The Origins of Totalitarianism*, 3 vols. (New York: Harcourt, Brace, 1951), 3:137–38.

28. Morton A. Reichek, "Storyteller," *New York Times Magazine*, 23 March 1975, 22.

29. *Plausible Prejudices: Essays on American Writing* (New York: W. W. Norton, 1985), 213.

30. *In My Father's Court* (New York: Farrar, Straus & Giroux, 1966), 68.

31. *Isaac Bashevis Singer and the Eternal Past* (New York: New York University Press, 1968), 121.

32. See, on this topic, Cynthia Ozick, "The Jewish Half-Genius," *Jerusalem Post International Edition*, 8 August 1978, 10–11.

33. *The Estate* (New York: Farrar, Straus & Giroux, 1969).

34. Marshall Breger and Bob Barnhart, "A Conversation with Isaac Bashevis Singer," in *Critical Views of Isaac Bashevis Singer*, ed. Irving Malin (New York: New York University Press, 1969), 42.

35. *Enemies, a Love Story* (New York: Farrar, Straus & Giroux, 1972).

36. "On Not Being a Dove," *Commentary* 87 (March 1989): 22–30.

37. *Middlemarch* (1871–72), chapter 20.

38. Quoted in *A Treasury of Yiddish Poetry*, ed. Irving Howe and Eliezer Greenberg (New York: Schocken Books, 1976), 53.

39. On 30 October 1988 I heard Singer (then eighty-four) address a group in Memphis. He told the assembled dinner guests that "it's true that you can never go home again, but it's good to be among my old friends from Warsaw tonight." Most, but not all, of his audience thought this a literary conceit.

Part 2

THE WRITER

Introduction

In his book on Singer's narrative strategies, David N. Miller argues that the author has turned his interviews (of which he has given hundreds) into a veritable genre of fiction. Miller shows how Singer dominates most of his interviewers to the point that he becomes "the controlling intellect and . . . author of his . . . interviews," thus making them into a literary form, the only one, moreover, in which Singer addresses his readers directly in English rather than in English translation from Yiddish.[1]

Although in his interviews Singer prefers to talk about himself rather than his work, I have confined my selections to those of his remarks which are immediately relevant to his philosophical and formal choices as a writer of fiction. The interviews excerpted here took place between 1963 and 1985.

In his interview with Blocker and Elman, Singer takes pains to dissociate himself from the Yiddish writer Sholem Asch, an immensely popular author in translation who was accused (as Singer has been) of writing for the English reader, even though he was writing in the Yiddish language. Singer then recalls how shocking to his parents, as to most religious Jews of their generation, was the idea of a secular literary vocation for a Jew. He expresses his usual skepticism about Jewish radical political movements, but exempts Zionism from his blanket condemnation, seeing in it "a great hope for the Jewish people." He abjures the title of moralist but insists that all literature of value comes from looking at life "from the eternal point of view of good and evil."

The interview with David Andersen and his colleagues brings out Singer's desire for an audience that lives next door to him, not only figuratively but literally. This interview specifies some of the writers of fiction who influenced Singer, apart from the Yiddish ones. We learn something of Singer's ideas about symbolism, about his use of narrators and reasons for choosing them as he does, and about his basing characters on actual persons. The interview ends with Singer stressing the importance of folklore in imaginative literature, even by self-conscious, sophisticated artists.

In his interview with Rosenblatt and Koppel, Singer asserts the power of the spiritual and the supernatural in his writing, as well as the unfathomable gap between human and divine intelligence. He maintains that art must be clannish and tribal rather than cosmopolitan, and accuses American Jewish writers of the shallowness that inevitably characterizes work composed in ignorance of Jewish history and tradition. He grants that his own work avoids characters born and bred in the United States because he must restrict his fiction to people whose history and inner life he knows intimately. Finally, Singer expresses hope that his books will serve as a bridge between assimilated young American Jews and "old Jewish life."

In his "dialogue" with Irving Howe, Singer tries to define himself as a Jewish writer rather than a Yiddish one. In reply, for example, to Howe's question about whether the dramatization of Singer's story "The Mirror" might owe something to the nonrealistic tradition of the Yiddish stage, Singer is quick to say no, and to insist that he was much more influenced by the cabalists and other "older writers." Singer gives as the main reason for his alienation from "the Yiddish tradition" its fondness for sentimentality and social justice, though he grudgingly allows that "Gimpel the Fool" has Yiddish literary antecedents. The other key point of the dialogue is Singer's explanation of his mixture of fascination and loathing for the Sabbatean tradition stemming from the seventeenth-century "false Messiah" Sabbatai Zevi. Singer links that tradition to modern political activism, against which he sets his stoical view that "the moment you begin to fight evil, you become a part of evil yourself."

In the excerpts from Singer's "conversations" with Richard Burgin, the author links his "externalizing" style of characterization with that of biblical narrative, where—or so he claims—we are always told what a person does or says, not what he or she thinks. Again, as in the Koppel-Rosenblatt interview, Singer castigates Marxist "cosmopolitanism" for undermining the rootedness in national culture essential to a genuine writer. His account of how he always bases his characters on real-life models—"I don't invent characters because the Almighty has already invented millions and billions of them"—gives the lie to assertions of some contemporary literary theorists (such as William Gass) that literary characters have no resemblance to actual persons. In the concluding segment Singer relates that not only the actors in his tales but even many of his narrators are based on real people (some of them his interviewers) whom Singer allows to tell their own stories in their own voices.

Note

1. David Neal Miller, *Fear of Fiction: Narrative Strategies in the Works of Isaac Bashevis Singer* (Albany: State University of New York Press, 1985), 103–5.

Interview (1963)

Interviewers: You don't at all have an image of someone reading you in a foreign language—English, for example?

Singer: That's a very important question. They accused Sholem Asch of writing for the translator. I don't say the accusation was true, but there were those who pointed to specific passages in Asch's work and said: "You see these lines. They were written for the English, not for the Yiddish reader." I take great care not to think about the reader in English or French or any other language. Nothing can spoil a writer more than writing for the translator. He must feel that he writes for people who know everything he knows—not for the stranger. It's only when you write for your own people and when you don't think about anybody else that the other people reading in a foreign language will appreciate your work and like it. Can you imagine Gogol writing for the French or the American reader? He was a Russian and wrote like a Russian and assumed that the reader knew everything he knew. You know, many of my Yiddish readers complain that I am too Jewish. They say: "We have already forgotten about all these things." "You remind us of things we would like to forget." But this doesn't bother me. I assume that the reader knows as much about Jewishness and Jewish life as I do.

Interviewers: How did your parents react to your wanting to be a writer?

Singer: It was a great shock to them. They considered all the secular writers to be heretics, all unbelievers—they really were too, most of them. To become a *literat* was to them almost as bad as becoming a *meshumed*, one who forsakes the faith. My father used to say that secular writers like Peretz were leading the Jews to heresy. He said everything they wrote was against God. Even though Peretz wrote in a religious vein, my father called his writing "sweetened poison," but poison

From Joel Blocker and Richard Elman, "An Interview with Isaac Bashevis Singer," *Commentary* 32 (November 1963): 364–72. Reprinted by permission of the American Jewish Committee.

nevertheless. And from his point of view he was right. Everybody who read such books sooner or later became a worldly man and forsook the traditions. In my family, of course, my brother had gone first and I went after him. For my parents, this was a tragedy.

Interviewers: About the time that you were growing up in Warsaw, Jewish radical movements of one sort or another had a very strong influence. Did you ever feel yourself attracted to any of these groups?

Singer: For some strange reason, just as I was skeptical about religious dogma, so was I skeptical about political dogmas. Certainly I was very close to these people, and maybe that was the trouble: you know, sometimes when you see the cook, the food doesn't seem very appetizing. When the ideologies sounded very attractive, I was close enough to see who was preaching them and how these people fought for power among themselves. The truth is, if you ask me, that the aches and troubles of this world cannot be cured by any system. Nevertheless, there are better and worse systems. Democracy seems to me to be one of the better systems, and there is no system which gives more power to the devil than Communism. As for Zionism, I always believed in it. I think that Israel is a great hope for the Jewish people. But it is true that just as I knew the socialist cooks, I knew some of the Zionist cooks in Poland. . . . Yet, in the case of Zionism, I felt that whoever the cook was, the food was wholesome. . . .

*

Interviewers: Are you familiar with Yeats's mysticism, with theosophy and Rosicrucianism?

Singer: No, I don't know Yeats. But I've read Madame Blavatsky. But let me come back to the literary reason for my use of the demonic and supernatural. First, it helps me to express myself. For example, by using Satan or a demon as a symbol, one can compress a great many things. It's a kind of spiritual stenography. It gives me more freedom. For another thing, the demons and Satan represent to me, in a sense, the ways of the world. Instead of saying this is the way things happen, I will say, this is the way demons behave. Devils symbolize the world for me, and by that I mean human beings and human behavior; and since I really believe in their existence—that is, not only symbolically but substantively—it is easy to see how this kind of literary style was born. I really love this style and I am always finding new symbols and new stories. I would say that every serious writer is possessed by certain

85

ideas or symbols, and I am possessed by my demons and they add a lot to my vision and my expression. . . .

*

Interviewers: What you're saying is that you are writing morality stories.

Singer: I would not characterize my stories as morality tales, but rather as being constructed around a moral point of view. It's true that when I write I don't look at the world as if it is beyond judgment. I do judge, not always explicitly, but more often implicitly. I even would go so far as to say that any writer who does not think in terms of good and evil cannot go very far in his writing. This is a tragedy in too much of modern writing; authors have ceased to look upon life from the eternal point of view of good and evil. They look upon life in a purely scientific way; they say that such circumstances create such people and such people behave so. The moment a writer begins to regard life from a behavioristic point of view, the writing falls flat and the writing descends to the level of his own characters. As the Talmud expresses it: *les din, les dayan*, there is no judgment and no judge. . . .

*

Interviewers: Of course you believe in God.

Singer: Yes, I do. I'm not, however, an observant Jew. I believe in God but not in man insofar as he claims God has revealed himself to him. . . . Consequently, I have no faith in dogmas of any kind; they are only the work of men. Man is born to free choice, to believe, to doubt, or to deny. I choose to believe. I also believe in the power of personal prayer. While I shun organized prayer and religion, I would call myself a religious man. The Higher Powers, I am convinced, are always with us, at every moment, everywhere, except, perhaps, at the meetings of Marxists and other left-wingers. There is no God there; they have passed a motion to that effect.

Interview (1970)

Interviewer: Of all the places in the United States I can't really imagine a writer living in the middle of Manhattan. Why do you live in that spot?

Singer: . . . Many of my readers live in Manhattan, at least the Yiddish readers. My newspaper *The Jewish Daily Forward* where I still contribute is in Manhattan, and many of my readers when they read a story of mine like to lift up the telephone and call me, and here they can call me—they don't have to make a long distance. For all these reasons I decided to live in Manhattan as long as it's possible.

Interviewer: Since you choose to write in Yiddish, can you speak about the future of the Yiddish language?

Singer: Yiddish is a sick language because the young people don't speak it. And many consider it a dead language. But in our history between being sick and dying is a long way.

Interviewer: You mentioned Poe and Shakespeare in your speech. What other writers in the English language have you read and enjoyed who might have influenced you?

Singer: When I was a boy I read Dickens. As a matter of fact—*The Pickwick [Papers]* I read in Hebrew. I until today don't know how it sounds in English. It sounded good in Hebrew, believe it or not. I also read *The Picture of Dorian Gray* in Hebrew, and Tolstoy and Dostoevski I read either in Hebrew, in Polish, in German. Edgar Allan Poe I read in Polish. And Shakespeare, "enlarged and improved," I read in Yiddish. It's only in my later years that I had to read Shakespeare without "improvement."

Interviewer: Were you influenced at all by the works of Sholom Aleichem?

From David M. Andersen, "Isaac Bashevis Singer: Conversations in California," *Modern Fiction Studies* 16 (Winter 1970–71): 424–39. ©1970 by Purdue Research Foundation, West Lafayette, Indiana. Reprinted by permission.

Singer: I was influenced more by Gogol than Sholom Aleichem. About two years ago they gave me to write a review about a collection of Gogol, a new translation. And when I read these stories I said to myself, "How is it possible that this man who has lived a hundred years before me has stolen so many of my stories."

Interviewer: When you write a story or a novel, is it based on people you know?

Singer: It is true I always rather take as a model a person whom I know. But it is never the same person because I combine all kinds of things. Sometimes I make from three people one person. Sometimes I take a person whom I met on Madison Avenue and decide he would fit very much to be in Lublin or Frampol. Because of this it happened to me that after the story was written I forgot who the model was. By the way, Frampol is a very small village in Poland. I remember that once a man came over to me and said to me, "You can bluff the whole world but not me." I said, "What is the matter?" He said, "I am from Frampol. You write always about sex and devils. I haven't seen neither sex nor devils in Frampol.". . .

*

Interviewer: How conscious should a writer be in the use of symbols in his work? Is it just talent that accounts for the kind of skill which you have in being able to blend symbolism and realism so that one doesn't become too labored or too obvious? Does it come spontaneously?

Singer: If a writer has a story to tell, if it's a good story, and he has a passion to write the story, he does not have to worry too much about the symbolism because a good story is always symbolic. When we read the stories in the Bible we feel that the writer did not try really to create symbolic stories. He just told a story about Adam and Eve and about Jacob and Rachel, and somehow they're all symbolic. But when a writer sits down with the idea of "writing symbolism," he will fail. Symbols often cancel out one another. If you will write ten symbols, one symbol will defy the other, and the net result may be nothing. So the best thing is: you tell a story or write a play and the symbol will be there anyhow. Or if you don't find it yourself, there will always be a critic who will find it. After I published *The Magician of Lublin*, I got a telephone call from a psychoanalyst, and he said, "I loved the way you made your hero go back to his mother's womb." It never occurred to me for a moment that the Magician of Lublin went back to his mother's womb, but I said to him, "Once a story is written it's not anymore my private property, and you are as entitled to find your interpretation as I am."

Interviewer: One of the ways that you handle that so beautifully is that you pick the narrator very carefully, or maybe it's just subconsciously right on your part.

Singer: I would say I use two kinds of narrators. Either I am the narrator myself, or it's an old woman. Because when I want to tell stories connected with folklore, I always let an old woman tell the story. Why I like narrators? There is a good reason for that: because when I write a story without a narrator I have to describe things, while if the narrator is a woman she can tell many things almost in one sentence. Because in life when you sit down to tell a story you don't act like a writer. You don't describe too much. You jump, you digress and this gives to the story speed and drama.

Interviewer: You mentioned the use of folklore in your stories, and, of course, old women would retain the folklore, but what do you think of the general movement away from folklore as a source of material for fiction, a movement which seems to have started with T. S. Eliot?

Singer: I think that it's a great tragedy that modern writing has divorced itself from folklore; because folklore is the best soil on which literature grows. Until about fifty years ago or so, literature was so deeply connected to folklore that we really didn't know where one ends and the other begins. It's the modern writer who has decided that we have enough of the folklore. Actually we are living in folklore, and we are creating folklore. We don't realize, for example, that psychoanalysis is going to be folklore fifty years from now. They will say these old-fashioned people believed that if you lie down on a couch you are going to be cured of many other things. Or our sociology will be folklore. We are all the time creating folklore; and because of this, there is no sense for a writer to run from it. There is no charm in literature without folklore. The fact that literature, the drama, has gone away from folklore is doing a lot of damage to modern art. This is my conviction. And I believe it is a gold mine which has never been exhausted and can never be exhausted.

Interview (1979)

Rosenblatt: Is there a vision as you look back on your work that you yourself, if you were to play critic on yourself, might—

Singer: Yes, there is a kind of vision in that. If I were to become for a moment a critic of my own writing, I would say that it always stresses the power of the spirit over the body in one way or another. I don't feel that life is nothing but a kind of chemical or physical accident, but there is always a plan behind it. I believe in Providence. I believe in spiritual powers, good and evil. The supernatural is always in my writing and somehow I always wanted to say to the reader that even though life looks to us chaotic, it is not as chaotic as we think. There is a scheme and a design behind it. But this is only one of many interpretations. This is my interpretation at this moment. I myself could find others in other moments or in other moods.

Rosenblatt: I believe you have described yourself at times as a pessimist. Wouldn't this kind of view—in terms of what our situation is today—really be an optimistic one since you say there is a design, a Providence—

Singer: Yes, I will tell you that I am a pessimist as far as our small world and our businesses are concerned, but I am not a pessimist as far as the universe is concerned. I am sure that the creator of the universe had a plan in it and that this plan was not a vicious plan. In other words, I believe in a good God, not a malicious God. But a good God can also make a lot of trouble to little beings who don't understand his design. I have two parakeets. They fly around free. They are not locked up in a cage. But if I want to move from one apartment to another and it's winter, I have to put them into a cage and cover the cage in the middle of the day so they don't catch a cold. But these parakeets don't know it. They see only cruelty. Suddenly I put them into a prison and I covered them. In the middle of the day I made

From *Isaac Bashevis Singer on Literature and Life: An Interview with Paul Rosenblatt and Gene Koppel* (Tucson: University of Arizona Press, 1979). Reprinted by permission.

darkness. From their point of view I am doing cruel things. From my point of view I am saving their lives because if I would carry them into the frost without a cover, they would catch cold or die. I have enough imagination to know that God may be much cleverer than I am. And since there is such a huge difference between the intelligence of a parakeet and mine, how huge is the difference between my intelligence and God's? . . .

*

Rosenblatt: Do you think that the writer of Yiddish by himself will create the demand on the part of young people for studying Yiddish?

Singer: There are very few writers of Yiddish nowadays. There are very few young ones. I don't build all my hopes on them, but I think that the writer generally, the Jewish writer, even though he may have mistaken theories, sooner or later will come—literature itself will compel him to come—to the conclusion that assimilation is poison from every point of view. It is certainly poison from the point of view of art, because art and assimilation are the very opposites. An artist is a person who is rooted in his milieu; he does not deny his parents and grandparents. In a way, art is clannish, but I mean in a positive way, not in a negative way. The person who wants to be a cosmopolitan is never an artist. There isn't such a thing as a cosmopolitan art; there isn't such a thing as a cosmopolitan drama or a cosmopolitan novel. If it is cosmopolitan, it is not a novel and it is not a drama. The real dramas of the world always take place among certain nations, certain people, in certain places and at certain times—they are very much concrete. From an artistic point of view, assimilation is a great misfortune, and the reason why Jewish-American literature hasn't reached more than it has reached is that this generation is still the victim of assimilation. . . .

Another thing, to be a Jewish writer you need more than to know just the Jewish people in the United States or in Chicago. It is necessary to know also more about the tradition. I would say that to be really called a Jewish writer you have to know Hebrew, you have to know Aramaic, you have to know the Talmud, history. In other words, it's not enough to know your hero. You must know the hero's father and grandfather and what they thought and how they behaved. Writers like Philip Roth and others know only one dimension. They cannot know their hero in depth, and this is the reason why some of them write such things as they do write. In my case, I know the American Jew's grandparents, but I don't know enough about the American Jews because I haven't lived in America long enough and I haven't been brought up in America. So all these are shortcomings but time will cure them. There will be an American-Jewish writer who will know both the present and the past and the languages and the tradition. I am sure that there will be such a writer.

Rosenblatt: Now you are working on some novels that take place here in America, aren't you?

Singer: Yes, I am. But the heroes of these novels are always immigrants. I never write about people who were born here. Once in awhile I will bring in an American, just for awhile. I will give him an episodic part, but I would never try to describe him in depth because when I write about a man I like not only to know the man and his parents and grandparents, but also what the man knows. I would never write about a chemist if I don't know chemistry. I would not write about a painter if I did not have a notion of painting. And since I don't know football and baseball and the many things an American born here does know and has experienced, I'm leery of writing about them. When I write about the immigrants from Poland I have the feeling that I know what they know. It is true that if a man happens to be a doctor this does not mean that I have to know medicine, but I know enough of doctors and their lives. Also, I would never make a doctor my protagonist. He would also be an episodic character. If you read my books you will see that I see to it that my characters are people whom I know thoroughly. I know what they are and I try to know what they know. Because of this it is a lot easier for me to write about a Polish rabbi or a Hasidic rabbi or a merchant in Warsaw, than, let's say, a lawyer in the United States, where I don't know really what kind of schooling he has and what the law is and what life in court looks like. I am very careful not to write about things of which I don't know or about which my knowledge is superficial. It is the worst thing a writer can do. . . .

*

Rosenblatt: Can we discuss the symbol for a moment? It seems today that every time we pick up a stone there is a symbol lurking underneath it.

Singer: Yes, some of the critics love to find symbolism in everything. It has become almost a sickness in modern criticism. Naturally every creator is by his very nature inclined to symbolism. Only in good writing the symbol comes out automatically. If there is a story, and if the story is genuine, there is always a symbol; you can even find many symbols if you look from different points of view. But in real writing the symbol is always the culmination of what is created, its climax. But if a man sits down and writes symbols into every line, it is boring; besides, one symbol soon cancels the other. The final result is an amalgamation of symbols which becomes nothing, which erases everything.

Take symbolism in the Bible. Every story in the Bible is a symbol —the story of Joseph, and the story of Abraham, and the story of Jacob, and so on—but this is not false symbolism. There is a story which sounds real, which makes sense, and the symbol is there anyhow. I once told a tailor in Poland to make for me a coat with crooked pockets. The tailor said to me, "You don't have to say 'crooked pockets'; you say straight pockets, they will come out crooked anyhow." If you sit down to write a good story it will be symbolic, but if you sit down and you begin to search in your mind for symbols, there will be no story and no symbolism. . . .

*

Rosenblatt: What about the future? What kind of hopes do you have for your work in the future?

Singer: Well, in my own case, what kind of hopes can I have? Either people will read *The Family Moskat* or *The Slave* one hundred years from now or they will not read them. Whatever they will do is all right with me. I don't think that these novels will redeem the world or help humanity get rid of sickness or of suppression or of any other things. I have only one hope, that I have given the children who were born in assimilated houses a certain bridge between themselves and old Jewish life. In other words, they will learn from my books how Jewish life was before assimilation, and how assimilation began. This is what they will learn. But this is not enough. They will also have to like the story. If the stories will not amuse them, they will not read them. They may be read by sociologists, but not by readers. But since I have given a lot of events, a lot of facts, and very little commentary, I hope that my works will not become as stale as those which are full of commentary.

Dialogue with Irving Howe (1973)

Singer: The truth is that the Yiddishists don't consider me a writer who writes in their tradition. Neither do I consider myself a writer in their tradition. I consider myself a writer in the Jewish tradition but not exactly the Yiddish tradition.

Howe: It would be worth taking a minute to explain what the distinction is in your mind between being in the Yiddish tradition on the one hand and in the Jewish tradition on the other hand.

Singer: The Yiddish tradition, in my mind, is a tradition of sentimentality and of social justice. These are the two pillars, so to speak, of the Yiddish kind of emotions. They are always for the underdog, very much so, and they are always sentimental. When I began to write I already felt that this kind of tradition is not in my character. I am not a sentimental person by nature. By sentimental, I mean really sentimental, let's call it schmaltz as it should be called. Neither is it my nature to fight for social justice although I am for social justice. But since I'm a pessimist and I believe that no matter what people are going to do it will always be wrong and there will never be any justice in this world, I have in my own way given up. And because of this I had to create my own kind of tradition.

Howe: So that, in creating your own tradition, you feel that you went back to sources in Jewish lore and in Jewish thought which precede historically the rise of Yiddish literature.

Singer: This is exactly how I feel because according to the Bible and even the Talmud, God really resented that He created man. The Bible keeps on repeating that one can expect very little from a human being, he is only blood and flesh and even if he tries to do good sometimes, it comes out wrong. I felt this way all my life.

Howe: This certainly comes through in a good many of your stories.

From Isaac Bashevis Singer and Irving Howe, "Yiddish Tradition vs. Jewish Tradition: A Dialogue," *Midstream* 19 (June/July 1973):33–38. Reprinted by permission of *Midstream*.

Yet the story of yours which perhaps is best known in America, "Gimpel the Fool," certainly can be seen as connected with parts of the Yiddish tradition. That story has a feeling for the underdog, for social justice, and there is also in that story the figure of "the sacred fool" who has appeared in the writings of a good many Yiddish writers like Peretz and others. Don't you think that that story has some connection?

Singer: I think so, you may be right. I think the reason for its special success may also be this, that it has the minimum schmaltz which some of our people demand.

Howe: On your general work as a Yiddish writer: the tradition that I myself have seen at work is a kind of underground tradition in the Jewish experience of the last few centuries, and that's the tradition which you struggle with and partly reject but it fascinates you. It's the tradition of false Messianism, the Sabbatean tradition, the tradition of Sabbatai Zevi which leads people to fanaticism, to hysteria, to disintegration, to explosion. *Satan in Goray* is very much concerned with this kind of tradition. It even comes through in some of your other stories less directly.

Singer: To me, Sabbatai Zevi was the symbol of the man who tries to do good and comes out bad. In other words, for me Sabbatai Zevi is in a way Stalin and all these people who tried so hard to create a better world and who ended up by creating the greatest misery. Naturally, Sabbatai Zevi couldn't have created as much misery as Stalin, he didn't have the power.

Howe: So that the whole tradition of Sabbatai Zevi is one which you see as part of the Faustian impulse of human beings to be active, to do things and then, afterwards, misery follows.

Singer: To fail, yes.

Howe: But that leads to the possibility that people would accuse you (and maybe some critics have) of a form of quietism, of believing that the best thing is to remain still in the world, not to act.

Singer: In a way, I'm not far from the Buddhist and the Indian way of thinking that the best thing you can do is run away from evil, not fight it, because the moment you begin to fight evil, you become a part of evil yourself.

Howe: That's the most interesting thing that's come out in a long time in regard to your own views. It certainly makes clear, although you write in Yiddish and have a marvelous Yiddish style, why the

Yiddishist writers feel that in some ways you are a stranger in their midst.

Singer: It is true. Yiddishism was very much influenced by socialism, Yiddishism is actually a very young movement. It's only about seventy or eighty years old. It was influenced by Karl Marx and by all the so-called social dogooders. Somehow, when I was young, I already saw the bad results of all these good deeds. I have seen young people go to Soviet Russia and disappear there. All these illusions and all these vain hopes. I compared them to the people who believed in Sabbatai Zevi, they were just as honest in their own way, just as zealous, and just as disappointed.

Interview (1985)

Singer: The truth is that we know what a person thinks, not by what he tells us, but by his actions. This reminds me—once a boy came to the *cheder* where I studied, and he said, "Do you know that my father wanted to box my ear?" So the teacher said, "How do you know that he wanted to box your ear?" And the boy said, "He did."

A man may sit for hours and talk about what he thinks, but what he really is, you can judge best by what he does. This is the real heresy in the psychoanalysis of our time where everything is measured by your thoughts and by your moods.

When you read the Bible, it never tells you what a man thought. It's always what he did. Take Genesis or the books of Joshua, Samuel, and Kings. David did this and Saul did this and Jonathan did this. There is one case in the Book of Esther where it says that "Haman said in his heart." So the Talmud says that this proves that the writer of the Book of Esther was inspired by the holy spirit, because if not, he would not have known what Haman was thinking in his heart. When you read Tolstoy and Flaubert and Chekhov, it's always what the hero or heroine said or did. I myself would never begin a story with, say, "Mr. So-and-So was sitting and thinking." I would rather describe how he looked, what he did and what he said. . . .

Singer: I don't think a Marxist has ever written a great book of fiction. This is because a writer must have roots and Marxism is against roots. A Marxist is a cosmopolitan or tries to be one, while a real writer belongs to his people, to his environment, whether he likes it or not. The cosmopolitan never writes anything unique. He is a generalizer. You can say of Gogol that he was politically naive or that he was a reactionary, but he stuck to his Ukrainian roots. The idea of roots is not to deny anything. You have to make the best of your origin and up-

From Isaac Bashevis Singer and Richard Burgin, *Conversations with Isaac Bashevis Singer* (New York: Doubleday, 1985), 53, 64–65, 78–79, 117. Reprinted by permission of Doubleday.

bringing. . . . You cannot write a love story of two human beings without dealing with their background—what nation they belonged to, what language their fathers spoke at home, and where they grew up. When you talk about a writer you always mention his nation, his language. Writers, more than any other artists, belong to their nation, their language, their history, their culture. They are both highly individualistic and highly attached to their origin. . . .

Singer: A number of writers make their short stories unusually long. Chekhov and Maupassant never did this. Their short stories were really *short*. Of course, it should have suspense from beginning to end. With bad writers the suspense begins to diminish almost immediately and then evaporates altogether. As for the process itself, first I get the idea or the emotion. Then I need a plot, a story with a beginning, a middle, and an end, just as Aristotle said it should be. A story to me must have some surprise. The plot should be such that when you read the first page, you don't know what the second will be. When you read the second page, you don't know what the third will be, because this is how life is, full of little surprises. The second condition is that I must have a passion to write the story. Sometimes I have a very good plot, but somehow the passion to write this story is missing. If this is the case, I would not write it.

And the third condition is the most important. I must be convinced, or at least have the illusion, that I am the only one who could write this particular story or this particular novel. Let's take, for example, "Gimpel the Fool." Another writer can write a hundred better stories, but the story of Gimpel the Fool, the way I tell it, is a story which only I could have written—not my colleagues or, say, writers who were brought up in English.

Now, for a plot you need characters. So instead of inventing characters, I contemplate the people whom I have met in my life who would fit into this story. I sometimes combine two characters and from them make one. I may take a person whom I met in this country and put him in Poland or vice versa. But just the same, I must have a model.

All real painters painted from models. They knew that Nature has more surprises than our imagination can ever invent. When you take a model, a character whom you know, you already attach yourself to Nature and all its surprises, idiosyncrasies, and peculiarities.

I don't invent characters because the Almighty has already invented millions and billions of them. Humanity may become a million years old and I'm sure that in all this time there will not be two people who are really alike. Experts at fingerprints do not create fingerprints. They learn how to read them. In the same way the writer reads human characters. . . .

Singer: I use the female narrator because among the Yiddish-speaking people the storytellers were either the Hassidim or the old women. They used to sit there on the porches of their houses and tell stories. And since they were not inhibited by special doubts, they would just say whatever they had to say in their own way and they said it sometimes in a very picturesque and remarkable manner. I usually use the monologue of some Hassid or of some old woman. Of course, in my stories, I also use monologues of people who come to ask "advice" from me. I often let people tell their stories in their own way, instead of my sitting there and telling their stories in my voice. It's both very convenient and very fruitful to let people tell their own stories.

Part 3

THE CRITICS

Introduction

The following selections, with the exception of the fierce, unkempt, and unbalanced piece by the poet Jacob Glatstein, have been chosen for their intrinsic quality, not for their representativeness. Singer's work has excited the interest of dozens of writers, exemplifying nearly every school of contemporary criticism, including that school whose predecessors Oscar Wilde referred to when he said that the real question about *Hamlet* was not whether the Prince of Denmark was mad or only pretending to be, but whether the critics of *Hamlet* were mad or only pretending to be. I have intentionally excluded from my selection two classes of Singer critics: those who know nothing of Yiddish literature or Jewish life and those who believe they know everything. The latter have constituted themselves as a coterie, forever stressing the unavailability of Singer's work to those who are not Yiddishists. They know so much about so little of Singer's work that they neither can be contradicted nor are worth contradicting.

Irving Howe's essay of 1966 is still the best general introduction to Singer's short fiction, an essay written by a critic who was instrumental in establishing Singer as a presence on the American literary scene. The essay stresses Singer's uniquely "reckless" surrender to the claims of imagination in writing about the destroyed world of Eastern European Jewry as if it were still alive. It offers a sophisticated account of the interaction between Singer's literary "modernism" and his involvement in Jewish faith, tradition, and history. Howe is also attuned to the extent to which Singer's characters break loose from their social milieu altogether and follow their individual destinies, toward heaven or hell. Yet it remains open to question whether, as Howe asserts, "Singer's ultimate concern is not with the collective experience of a chosen or martyred people but with the enigmas of personal fate."

Ruth Wisse's fine essay, written on the occasion of Singer's winning the Nobel Prize in literature, recounts, from the perspective of a specialist in Yiddish literature, Singer's progress as a professional writer.

Wisse narrates his career from its beginnings in Warsaw, the capital of Yiddish culture, in the twenties, the heyday of Yiddish literature. She shows how deeply embedded Singer was in the literary ambience from which he has often affected alienation. Wisse also examines the relation between Singer's unusually "old-fashioned" family background and the genesis of his fiction, which so often treats the conflict between Jewish tradition and worldliness. She pays particular attention to the influence of Singer's older brother, Israel Joshua, who transmitted enough of his secularism to change Isaac from a yeshiva student to a writer, but not enough of his leftism to dilute the young man's skepticism about socialist utopianism. The main thrust of Wisse's essay is to show that Singer still "remains surprisingly true to his earliest literary ideals."

Although Irving Feldman's essay was formally only a review of *The Spinoza of Market Street*, it offers striking general observations on the pervasive qualities of Singer's art. Feldman is struck by the way in which the world of the shtetl springs forth from Singer's pages as something at once real and more than real. He tries to define "the almost perfect externality" of Singer's style, his ability to render "inward" states in concrete images, details, and actions; and he argues that all Singer's technical brilliance is employed in the service of one overriding theme: "the extraordinary fragility of the cosmic order, the way in which the world is sustained on a pinpoint of grace."

Cynthia Ozick's dazzling story "Envy; or, Yiddish in America" captures the world of the Yiddish writers in America in the aftermath of the Holocaust, and especially the jealousy of Singer's success among other Yiddish writers. In this story the character named Ostrover is modeled on Singer; the writer named Edelshtein upon the poet Jacob Glatstein. The first excerpt recounts Singer's successful career from the point of view of his enemies; the second excerpt is a comic version of a typical public appearance by Singer before an adoring audience.

The most hostile of the critical verdicts on Singer reproduced here was written by Singer's fellow Yiddish writer, Jacob Glatstein. Glatstein was a poet of great distinction, who produced a body of work about the Holocaust that is unsurpassed in any language. Cynthia Ozick's story suggests that the ill feeling that existed between the two writers was based partly on Glatstein's resentment of the popularity that Singer gained through being translated into English, but also on their differing evaluations of Yiddish. Singer wrote (and writes) in Yiddish; but Glatstein *believed* in Yiddish. In the wake of the Holocaust, Yiddish had become for Glatstein the language of martyrdom, a new holy tongue displacing Hebrew from that role. Singer's use of Yiddish to treat "horror and eroticism" was in Glatstein's eyes an act of sacrilege.

Irving Howe

No other living writer has yielded himself so completely and recklessly as has Isaac Bashevis Singer to the claims of the human imagination. Singer writes in Yiddish, a language that no amount of energy or affection seems likely to save from extinction. He writes about a world that is gone, destroyed with a brutality beyond historical comparison. He writes within a culture, the remnant of Yiddish in the Western world, that is more than a little dubious about his purpose and stress. He seems to take entirely for granted his role as a traditional storyteller speaking to an audience that values story-telling both in its own right and as a binding communal action—but also, as it happens, an audience that keeps fading week by week, shrinking day by day. And he does all this without a sigh or apology, without so much as a Jewish groan. It strikes one as a kind of inspired madness: here is a man living in New York City, a sophisticated and clever writer, who composes stories about places like Frampol, Bilgoray, Kreshev, *as if they were still there*. His work is shot through with the bravado of a performer who enjoys making his listeners gasp, weep, laugh and yearn for more. Above and beyond everything else he is a great performer, in ways that remind one of Twain, Dickens, Sholom Aleichem.

Singer writes Yiddish prose with a verbal and rhythmic brillance that, to my knowledge, can hardly be matched. When Eliezer Greenberg and I were working on our *Treasury of Yiddish Stories*, he said to me: "Singer has to be heard, to be believed." Behind the prose there is always a spoken voice, tense, ironic, complex in tonalities, leaping past connectives. Greenberg then read to me, with a fluency and pith I could never capture in my own reading of Yiddish, Singer's masterpiece, *Gimpel the Fool*, and I knew at once (it took no great powers of judgment) that here was the work of a master. The story came as a stroke of revelation, like a fiction by Babel or Kleist encountered for the first time.

From the introduction to *Selected Short Stories of Isaac Bashevis Singer*, ed. Irving Howe. (New York: Random House, 1966), i–xxvi. © 1966 by Random House, Inc. Reprinted by permission of Random House, Inc.

Singer's stories claim attention through their vivacity and strangeness of surface. He is devoted to the grotesque, the demonic, the erotic, the quasi-mystical. He populates his alien sub-world with imps, devils, whores, fanatics, charlatans, spirits in seizure, disciples of false messiahs. A young girl is captured by the spirit of a dead woman and goes to live with the mourning husband as if she were actually his wife; a town is courted and then shattered by a lavish stranger who turns out to be the devil; an ancient Jew suffering unspeakable deprivations during the first World War, crawls back to his village of Bilgoray and fathers a son whom, with marvellous aplomb, he names Isaac. Sometimes the action in Singer's stories follows the moral curve of traditional folk tales, with a charming, lightly-phrased "lesson" at the end; sometimes, the spiral of a quizzical modern awareness; at best, the complicated motions of the old and the contemporary yoked together, a kind of narrative double-stop.

Orgiastic lapses from the moral order, pacts with the devil, ascetic self-punishments, distraught sexuality occupy the foreground of Singer's stories. Yet behind this expressionist clamour there is glimpsed the world of the *shtetl*, or East European Jewish village, as it stumbled and slept through the last few centuries. Though Singer seldom portrays it fullface, one must always keep this world in mind while reading his stories: it forms the base from which he wanders, the norm from which he deviates but which controls his deviation. And truly to hear these stories one must have at least a splinter of knowledge about the culture from which Singer comes, the world he continues to evoke as if it were still radiantly alive: the Hasidim still dancing, the rabbis still pondering, the children still studying, the poor still hungering as if it had not all ended in ashes and death. . . .

Isaac Bashevis Singer is the only living Yiddish writer whose translated work has caught the imagination of a Western (the American) literary public. Though the settings of his stories are frequently strange, the contemporary reader—for whom the determination not to be shocked has become a point of honor—is likely to feel closer to Singer than to most other Yiddish writers. Offhand this may be surprising, for Singer's subjects are decidedly remote and exotic: in *Satan in Goray* the orgiastic consequences of the false messianism of seventeenth-century East European Jewish life; in *The Magician of Lublin* a portrait of a Jewish magician–Don Juan in late nineteenth-century Poland who exhausts himself in sensuality and ends as a penitent ascetic; in his stories a range of demonic, apocalyptic, and perversely sacred moments of *shtetl* life. Yet one feels that, unlike many of the Yiddish writers who treat more familiar and up-to-date subjects, Singer commands a distinctly "modern" sensibility.

Now this is partly true—in the sense that Singer has cut himself off from some of the traditional styles and assumptions of Yiddish writing. But it is also not true—in the sense that any effort to assimilate Singer to literary "modernism" without fully registering his involvement with Jewish faith and history is almost certain to distort his meanings.

Those meanings, one might as well admit, are often enigmatic and hard to come by. It must be a common experience among Singer's readers to find a quick pleasure in the caustic surfaces of his prose, the nervous tokens of his virtuosity, but then to acknowledge themselves baffled as to his point and purpose. That his fiction does have an insistent point and stringent purpose no one can doubt: Singer is too ruthlessly single-minded a writer to content himself with mere slices of representation or displays of the bizarre. His grotesquerie must be taken seriously, perhaps as a recoil from his perception of how irremediably and gratuitously ugly human life can be. He is a writer completely absorbed by the demands of his vision, a vision gnomic and compulsive but with moments of high exaltation; so that while reading his stories one feels as if one were overhearing bits and snatches of monologue, the impact of which is both notable and disturbing, but the meaning withheld.

Now these are precisely the qualities that the sophisticated reader, trained to docility before the exactions of "modernism," has come to applaud. Singer's stories work, or prey, upon the nerves. They leave one unsettled and anxious, the way a rationalist might feel if, waking at night in the woods, he suddenly found himself surrounded by a swarm of bats. Unlike most Yiddish fiction, Singer's stories neither round out the cycle of their intentions nor posit a coherent and ordered universe. They can be seen as paradigms of the arbitrariness, the grating injustice, at the heart of life. They offer instances of pointless suffering, dead-end exhaustion, inexplicable grace. And sometimes, as in Singer's masterpiece, *Gimpel the Fool*, they turn about, refusing to rest with the familiar discomforts of the problematic, and drive towards a prospect of salvation on the other side of despair, beyond soiling by error or will. This prospect does not depend on any belief in the comeliness or lawfulness of the universe; whether God is there or not, He is surely no protector: "He had worked out his own religion [Singer writes about one of his characters]. There was a Creator, but He revealed himself to no one, gave no indications of what was permitted or forbidden." Things happen, the probable bad and improbable good, both of them subject to the whim of the fortuitous; and the sacred fools like Gimpel, perhaps they alone, learn to roll with the punch, finding the value of their life in a total passivity and credulousness, a complete openness to suffering.

Singer's stories trace the characteristic motions of human destiny: a heavy climb upward ("The Old Man"), a rapid tumble downward ("The Fast"). Life forms a journeying to heaven and hell, mostly hell. What determines the direction a man will take? Sometimes the delicate manoeuvres between his will and desire, sometimes the heat of his vanity, sometimes the blessing of innocence. But more often than not, it is all a mystery which Singer chooses to present rather than explain. As his figures move upward and downward, aflame with the passion of their ineluctable destiny, they stop for a moment in the *shtetl* world. Singer is not content with the limitations of materiality, yet not at all indifferent to the charms and powers of the phenomenal universe. In his calculus of destiny, however, the world is a resting-place and what happens within it, even within the social enclave of the Jews, is not of lasting significance. Thick, substantial, and attractive as it comes to seem in Singer's representation, the world is finally but lure and appearance, a locale between heaven and hell, the shadow of larger possibilities.

In most Yiddish fiction the stress is quite different. There the central "character" is the collective destiny of the Jews in *galut* or exile; the central theme, the survival of a nation deprived of nationhood; the central ethic, the humane education of men stripped of worldly power yet sustained by the memory of chosenness and the promise of redemption. In Singer the norm of collective life is still present, but mostly in the background, as a tacit assumption; his major actions break away from the limits of the *shtetl* ethic, what has come to be known as *Yiddishkeit*, and then move either backward to the abandon of false messianism or forward to the doubt of modern sensibility. (There is an interesting exception, the story called "Short Friday," which in its stress upon family affection, ritual properties and collective faith, approaches rather closely the tones of traditional Yiddish fiction.)

The historical settings of East European Jewish life are richly presented in Singer's stories, often not as orderly sequences in time but as simultaneous perceptions jumbled together in the consciousness of figures for whom Abraham's sacrifice, Chmielnicki's pogroms, the rise and fall of Hasidism and the stirrings of the modern world are all felt with equal force. Yet Singer's ultimate concern is not with the collective experience of a chosen or martyred people but with the enigmas of personal fate. Given the slant of his vision, this leads him to place a heavy reliance upon the grotesque as a mode of narration, even as an avenue towards knowledge. But the grotesque carries with it a number of literary and moral dangers, not the least being the temptation for Singer to make it into an end in itself, which is to say, something facile and sensationalistic. In his second-rank stories he falls back a little too comfortably upon the devices of which he is absolute master, like a magician supremely confident his tricks will continue to work. But mainly the grotesque succeeds in Singer's stories because it comes to symbolise meaningful digressions from a cultural norm. An unin-structed reader may absorb Singer's grotesquerie somewhat too easily into the assumptions of modern literature; the reader who grasps the ambivalence of Singer's relation to Yiddish literature will see the gro-tesquerie as a cultural sign by means of which Singer defines himself against his own past.

It is hardly a secret that in the Yiddish literary world Singer is re-garded with a certain suspicion. His powers of evocation, his resources as a stylist are acknowledged, yet many Yiddish literary persons, in-cluding the serious ones, seem uneasy about him. One reason is that "modernism"—which, as these people regard Singer, signifies a heavy stress upon sexuality, a concern for the irrational, expressionist distor-tions of character, and a seeming indifference to the humane ethic of Yiddishism—has never won so strong a hold in Jewish culture as it has in the cultures of most Western countries. For the Yiddish writers, "modernism" has been at best an adornment of manner upon a subject inescapably traditional.

The truly "modern" writer, however, is not quite trustworthy in relation to his culture. He is a shifty character by choice and need, unable to settle into that solid representativeness which would allow him to act as a cultural "spokesman." And to the extent that Singer does share in the modernist outlook he must be regarded with distrust by Yiddish readers brought up on such literary "spokesmen" as Peretz, Abraham Reisen, and H. Leivick. There is no lack of admiration among Yiddish readers for Singer's work: anyone with half an ear for the cadence and idiom of that marvellous language must respond to his prose. Still, it is a qualified, a troubled admiration. Singer's moral outlook, which seems to move with equal readiness towards the sensational and the ascetic, is hardly calculated to put Yiddish readers at their ease. So they continue to read him, with pleasure and anxiety.

And as it seems to me, they are not altogether wrong. Their admiring resistance to Singer's work may constitute a more attentive and serious response to his iconoclasm than the gleeful applause of those who read him in English translation and take him to be another writer of "black comedy," or heaven help us, a mid-twentieth-century "swinger." . . .

Using demons and imps as narrators proves to be a wonderful device for structural economy: they replace the need to enter the "inner" life of the characters, the whole plaguing business of the psychology of motives, for they serve as symbolic equivalents and co-ordinates to human conduct, what Singer calls a "spiritual stenography." In those stories, however, where Singer celebrates the power of human endurance, as in *The Little Shoemakers* and *The Old Man*, he uses third person narrative in the closest he comes to a "high style," so that the rhetorical elevation will help to create an effect of "epical" sweep.

Within his limits Singer is a genius. He has total command of his imagined world; he is original in his use both of traditional Jewish materials and his modernist attitude towards them; he provides a serious if enigmatic moral perspective; and he is a master of Yiddish prose. Yet there are times when Singer seems to be mired in his own originality, stories in which he displays a weakness for self-imitation that is disconcerting. Second-rate writers imitate others, first-rate writers themselves, and it is not always clear which is the more dangerous.

Having gone this far, we must now turn again. If Singer's work can be grasped only on the assumption that he is crucially a "modernist" writer, one must add that in other ways he remains profoundly subject to the Jewish tradition. And if the Yiddish reader is inclined to slight the "modernist" side of his work, any other reader is likely to underestimate the traditional side.

One of the elements in the Jewish past that has most fascinated Singer is the recurrent tendency to break loose from the burden of the Mosaic law and, through the urging of will and ecstasy, declare an end to the *galut*. Historically, this has taken the form of a series of messianic movements, one led in the seventeenth century by Sabbatai Zevi and another in the eighteenth by Jacob Frank. The movement of Sabbatai

Zevi appeared after the East European Jewish community had been shattered by the rebellion-pogrom of the Cossack chieftain, Chmielnicki. Many of the survivors, caught up in a strange ecstacy that derived all too clearly from their total desperation, began to summon apocalyptic fantasies and to indulge themselves in long-repressed religious emotions which, perversely, were stimulated by the pressures of Cabbalistic asceticism. As if in response to their yearnings, Sabbatai, a pretender rising in the Middle East, offered to release them of everything that rabbinical Judaism had confined or suppressed. He spoke for the tempting doctrine that faith is sufficient for salvation; for the wish to evade the limits of mundane life by forcing a religious transcendence; for the union of erotic with mystical appetites; for the lure of a demonism which the very hopelessness of the Jewish situation rendered plausible. In 1665–66 Sabbatianism came to orgiastic climax, whole communities, out of a conviction that the messiah was in sight, discarding the moral inhibitions of exile. Their hopes were soon brutally disappointed, for Sabbatai, persecuted by the Turkish Sultan, converted to Mohammedanism. His followers were thrown into confusion and despair, and a resurgent rabbinism again took control over Jewish life. Nevertheless, Sabbatianism continued to lead an underground existence among the East European Jews—even (I have been told by *shtetl* survivors) into the late nineteenth and twentieth century. It became a secret heretical cult celebrating Sabbatai as the apostate saviour who has been required to descend to the depths of the world to achieve the heights of salvation.

To this buried strand of Jewish experience Singer has been drawn in fascination and repulsion, portraying its manifestations with great vividness and its consequences with stern judgment. It is a kind of experience that rarely figures in traditional Yiddish writing yet is a significant aspect of the Jewish past. Bringing this material to contemporary readers, Singer writes *in* Yiddish but often quite apart from the Yiddish tradition; indeed, he is one of the few Yiddish writers whose relation to the Jewish past is not determined or screened by that body of values we call Yiddishism.

Ruth R. Wisse

The award to Isaac Bashevis Singer of the Nobel Prize for Literature brings to a climax the most fortunate career in modern Yiddish letters. With deference to Singer's demons, it would be only proper to spit three times upon such provocation, and to dispel their impish envy with the formula, may no evil eye behold him. But the occasion should be marked for rejoicing, especially since the decline of the language in which Singer writes, the destruction of his community, and the thwarted fate of many of his fellow Yiddish writers have so often required the compassionate tones of mourning.

The emphasis on loss and decline may seem inevitable in any discussion of Bashevis Singer's work: the gloom is in either the subject or the writer, or both. Idyllic stories of the East European *shtetl*, like "Short Friday" or "The Little Shoemakers," vivify a world whose beatific fictional existence is set into fiercely tragic perspective by its historical extinction. Most of Singer's stories inspire a fresh awareness of human malignancy and remorseless fate. The author's fatalism is prominent in large novels, like *The Family Moskat*, which trace the disintegration of modern Jewish society through a series of characters who gravitate unerringly toward their doom. As Singer has often remarked, the pessimist is the realist. His unblinking realistic eye has noted this century's unholy marvels, including those special revelations it has offered the Jew.

Yet the progress of Singer as a professional writer is an unusually happy study. His first published story, submitted under a pseudonym to the literary contest of a Warsaw weekly in 1925 when he was twenty-one, was a prizewinning entry.[1] A year later he was the youngest of forty-six contributors to the massive anthology, *Warshever Shriftn*, establishing his literary presence among the major Yiddish writers of his period. His first novel, *Satan in Goray*, published serially in a local magazine, was issued in book form by the Library of the Yiddish PEN

From "Singer's Paradoxical Progress," *Commentary* 67 (February 1979). 33–38. Reprinted by permission of American Jewish Committee.

Club in 1935, the first volume of what was to have become a series of annual stellar publications. Singer had the prescience and good fortune to leave Warsaw in the mid 1930s for New York, where, after a period of dislocation, he became a regular contributor to the *Jewish Daily Forward*, the only moderately secure affiliation ever afforded to the Yiddish writer. He was able, on the *Forward*, to cultivate two literary voices—that of "Warshavsky," the feuilletonist and personal chronicler, and that of "Bashevis," the writer and novelist—finding for each an appreciative audience. Lastly, and by no means least, he was "discovered" in the early 1950s by Irving Howe, the editors of *Commentary* and *Partisan Review*, and the late Cecil Hemley of the Noonday Press, and set aloft on the wave of fame that nowhere swells so high and fast as in America. The Nobel Prize for Literature confers international recognition and honor upon a writer who has gone "from strength to strength."

More compelling than the story of his reputation is that of Singer's literary progress. Though he presents himself to his American audiences as a rather puckish character, musing about demons, asking for explanations of a difficult term like "modernism," parrying with quips and aphorisms the questions addressed to him as if to an oracle, Singer is really a thoroughly professional literary man who has carefully considered the nature of his craft. Plunged into the thick of Jewish cultural life in his late adolescence, he served an excellent artistic apprenticeship, becoming one of the first and few Yiddish writers to make his living—meager though it sometimes was—solely by the pen.

Bashevis Singer became a writer in the heyday of Yiddish literature in the 1920's at what was undoubtedly its geographic center: Warsaw, capital of the new Republic of Poland, a city whose 300,000 Jews constituted about one-third of the total population. The classical period of Yiddish literature had come to a sudden end with World War I, when the three giants—I. L. Peretz, Sholem Aleichem, and Mendele Mocher Sforim—died in rapid succession between 1915 and 1917. Under Peretz's guiding and often autocratic rule—his disciples called him their "rebbe"—his home in Warsaw had become the heart of a spirited cultural renaissance. Although emigration and shifting political borders in the postwar years greatly affected Jewish demography, Warsaw remained the mecca of Yiddish letters until the 1939 German invasion.

When Singer first began to publish in 1925, there were in Warsaw a number of important Yiddish dailies, representing the spectrum of

Jewish ideologies and a considerable journalistic range from photo-express sensationalism to high-quality coverage and editorial analysis. Singer found employment with *Literarische Bleter*, the most prestigious literary weekly ever published in Yiddish. He was soon a full-fledged member of the Union of Jewish Writers and Journalists, which boasted a membership of about 300 professionals, sponsored hundreds of literary evenings, published its own anthologies, and provided an around-the-clock meeting place for discussion and drink. To be a Yiddish writer in Warsaw, said the poet, Melekh Ravitch, when he arrived there from Vienna after World War I, was "to feel the Redemption at hand, and to be at its center."

In addition to being well situated for a literary debut in Yiddish, Singer also witnessed in his own family a microcosmic drama of the conflict between Jewish tradition and worldliness, which was the main subject and stimulus of modern Jewish writing. Few writers, whether in Hebrew or Yiddish, have emerged from so thoroughly "old fashioned" and learned a home. As Singer himself has explained, the Jewish *shtetl* of Poland experienced the Enlightenment, the *Haskalah*, much later and with greater suddenness than did similar communities of Russia and Lithuania, where so many Jewish writers had originated: "Until 1914 most *shtetlakh* in Poland remained observant (*frum*). Jews lived as they had hundreds of years earlier. . . . The Enlightenment as a mass movement came to Poland with World War I, and because of its delay and momentum, assumed almost epidemic proportions. The revolution in Russia, the arrival of the Germans and the Austrians, the creation of the Polish Republic, the Balfour Declaration—all of this had a simultaneous impact. Processes that elsewhere lasted several decades here transpired virtually overnight."[2]

Singer's first-hand familiarity with the "pre-Enlightenment" Polish *shtetl* and his upbringing in a bookish as well as a pious home gave him immediate access to Jewish folkways and literary sources from which Jewish writers, even of the preceding generation, had felt themselves rather removed. Back in the 1890s, I. L. Peretz and his friends were already collecting from outlying areas folk materials that could be re-worked in modern literary forms. Some of the impetus for S. An-ski's haunting drama, *The Dybbuk*, derived from the ethnographic expedition that the author had undertaken to gather materials thought to be in danger of disappearing. As Singer has described his home, much of this endangered lore was the daily stuff of his life, his for the taking.

If his parents, a small-town rabbi and rabbi's daughter, and the various visiting and visited relatives remained a wellspring of tradition, Singer's older sister, Esther, and his brother, Israel Joshua, soon introduced the challenge of secular modernity. Israel Joshua, a draft evader during the war for reasons of conscience, was caught up by the excitement of the Bolshevik revolution and began his literary career under its spell. Later in Warsaw, he was a prominent companion of "The Gang" (*Di Khaliastre*), a determinedly innovative group of Yiddish writers who took as their bible the *Ethics* of Spinoza, and as their literary model the expressionistic bravado of the Russian poet, Mayakovsky. Before Bashevis Singer attempted the passage from home, his older brother had already publicly rejected the Jewish God and braved the heady atmosphere of the artistic world. Of the clashes between generations in his home, Singer was to say: "Although later in my life I read a great deal of philosophy, I never found more compelling arguments than those that came up in my own kitchen."

While the example of Israel Joshua no doubt facilitated the transition of young Isaac from *Yeshiva bokher* to Yiddish writer, it also preempted some of the younger writer's independent initiative in this direction. In order to step out on his own, Bashevis had not only to reject the assumptions of his parents, but also those of his brother who was intimidatingly talented and famous. It was necessary to separate himself from both his home and from the new "revolutionary" circles in which his brother played such a prominent role. And, in fact, though Singer fell in with some trends of his day—the naturalistic impulse to show the seamy side of life and to emphasize its sexuality; the attraction to Spinoza, vegetarianism, pacifism—he was among the very few to oppose political ideologies, whether nationalist or socialist. Even more solitary was his opposition to literary modernism as a means of expressing the unease and disjunction of the 1920s. His earliest published story, about a man's precipitous decline, ends in a shocking scene: the ailing father is asked by his daughter, a prostitute, to roll over in bed so that she might use its other half for her trade. This was certainly an attack on the values of modesty in which Singer was raised. At the same time, the spare, direct narrative style of this and all the rest of his work repudiated current vogues of impressionism and expressionism, while the emphasis on character rather than social conditioning called into question all faiths in a new world order.

His position between the contending values of a traditional past and an ideologically-impelled future seems to have endowed Singer with a curious detachment, curious certainly within the mainstream of Jewish literature which took any number of directions but was invariably *engagé*. More onlooker than participant, Singer has seen the forces of opposing ideas canceling one another out, much as in his works the charm of one beloved is soon deflected by the lure of another and then, invariably, by yet a third. Singer has referred to himself as "unsentimental." He did not nurse ideals that could be shattered, or trust the human condition enough to believe in ultimate remedies. The habit of skepticism, though it has sometimes chilled Singer's work to the bone, made him an exceptionally steady recording secretary for his times.

From the outset, Singer defined his craft not in terms of possibilities but in terms of limitations. In the manner of a proper *halakhic* Jew, he first set up the fence of restrictions before exploring the opportunities within its bounds. Though he has experimented in a number of genres over the years, and expanded his two original locales, the old world and the new, to include a third, the beyond, he remains surprisingly true to his earliest literary ideals.

For Bashevis Singer, literature is realism and realism demands a narrative that depicts and speaks for itself. "The description, the given fact, was always the attribute of the realistic narrative," wrote Singer in a 1927 essay, "just as sentiment and mood are dominant in the lyric."[3] The poet may *react* to events, but the prose realist sets up the events themselves, leaving reaction to the reader. The fiction writer is sentenced to details, and "the subtler the intended mood, the more details . . . he must artfully combine." The realist must deal with objective facts; only in dialogue, in the exchange of voices, do we have a "tiny window" into the unseen inner life of the characters.

Singer's endorsement of realism is in large measure an attack upon the moderns, particularly the expressionists, who wished "to tear down all barriers and penetrate directly to the very essence." He considers their exhibitionistic art intrinsically inferior to that of the consistent realist like himself, who accepts the binding limitations of narration as the first condition of success. "In graphic form it isn't possible to render everything, but everything in a realistic narrative must be given graphic form."

While submitting to its restraints, Singer raises some traditional objections to realism which also express his own impatience. Can objective descriptions really communicate the full complexity of the individual? What about the intellectual who thinks more than he acts: can realism do him justice, or must it favor the folk type? Is there no other direct source for the artist apart from the natural world, apprehended through the senses? These questions clearly anticipate the author's attempted solutions. Like the libertines of his stories who require a social context of propriety, Singer defines a thoroughly conservative norm which he may then bedevil and transgress.

He soon began to use historical chronicles, folk tales, and the supernatural to explore those subjects and ideas that could not be treated with sufficient freedom in contemporary realistic settings. His "chronicles" do obey the laws of objective narration, his imps are kept dutifully subject to the same laws of fiction that govern their human victims. Yet in these stories, the very normalcy of the form undercuts the assumptions of materialism and natural reason on which literary realism rests. Erotic impulses and subconscious desires are embodied in androgynous, lesbian, sadistic, and murderous creatures whose substantive existence is portrayed in such "authentic" and charming detail of language and setting that they seem not only real, but commonplace. The apparent simplicity of Singer's narrative form, like the innocence of his characters, is only the better to call them into question with.

Notes

1. For this interesting detail, I am indebted to Khone Shmeruk's introduction to *Der shpigl un andere dertseylungen*, a collection of Singer's first-person narratives, issued by the Hebrew University, 1975.

2. *"Arum der yidisher literatur in poyln"* ("Concerning Yiddish Literature in Poland"), *Zukunft*, August 1943.

3. *"Verter oder bilder"* ("Words or Images") in *Literarishe Bleter*, 1927, no. 34.

Irving Feldman

Mr. Singer's obvious mastery aside, what is anomalous is that his fiction seems to emerge from a lived world and his art to be no more than a description of the physics and atmosphere of this world. Perhaps this is what makes Mr. Singer's fiction both so lucid and impenetrable, for when an art is based on a real world, setting and surface become concrete, decisive. And yet—the greatest of rarities—it is something more than "real." Surely, the East European Jewish hamlet, the *shtetl*, never existed so purely as Mr. Singer gives it to us, as special and crystalline a thing as any fully created artistic world. And he can write of it only from memory and dream, for it is dead and gone forever. "Lived," "real," "more than real," "fully created"—this is only to say that, with all its religious aspiration and social and cultural abasement, the *shtetl* is, clearly, for Mr. Singer a powerfully desired world, and his writing is quick with the verve, wit, precision, and crispness possible only to passion. It would be no easy task to find anything comparable to this in contemporary literature.

And further. From any modern point of view Mr. Singer's *shtetl* is an anachronism: superstitious, disenfranchised, impoverished, totally saturated with its religion, isolated, ignorant of all save the holy scriptures, poised between the timeless round of custom and ritual and the eternal Law, swept by mass hysteria, terrorized and living in the memory of terror and the hope of deliverance, divided by fierce sectarian quarrels, distrustful, narrow in its purview, grandiose in its expectations, forgotten—this is Mr. Singer's deeply medieval *shtetl* the Enlightenment never touched. His treatment of this world is no less singular, without the slightest hint of the *faux naif*, of a fetching after "folk quality" or the exotic.

It seems to me that the key to Mr. Singer's success is the almost perfect externality of his style. There is so little inwardness, pathos, emotional lingering in his characters who seem, continually, to exter-

From "The Shtetl World," *Kenyon Review* 24, no.1 (Winter 1962): 173–77. © 1962 by Kenyon College. Reprinted by permission.

nalize themselves in cries and gestures. If, for example, a young girl in love is described, the inward part of her emotion is given cursorily but her behavior is given in detail. Again, when a Singer character undergoes some crisis of faith, he does not feel continuously through it; rather his mind is flooded with streams of images, maxims, arguments—that is, with fragments of the world external to him. So, too, Mr. Singer's characteristic stylistic device is the bright, rapid catalogue. Indeed, the stunning "Black Wedding" in this volume is little more than an extended catalogue of the tortures of the mad Hindele: "But horror of horrors, Hindele became pregnant. A devil grew inside her. She could see him through her own belly as through a cobweb: half-frog, half-ape, with eyes of a calf and scales of a fish. He ate her flesh, sucked her blood, scratched her with his claws, bit her with his pointed teeth. . . . His skull was of copper, his mouth of iron. He had capricious urges. He told her to eat lime from a wall, the shell of an egg." Or, here is Glicka, one of the liars in "A Tale of Two Liars":

> True, she was no beauty. Her nose sloped like a ram's horn, but she did have a pleasantly pale complexion, and large, dark eyes; in addition, her chin was pointed and her tongue glib. There was bounce to her walk, and she scattered witticisms wherever she went.
> No matter what occurred, she could remember a similar experience; for every sorrow, she offered comfort, for every illness, a remedy. She was dazzling in her high-buttoned shoes, woolen dress, fringed silk shawl, and head-band festooned with precious gems.

Unqualified by any subjectivity, each item in these catalogues seems to hold forth its pristine savor, to announce its quality with the same glamor things demonstrate in the Bible or in Homer. This vision of things is curiously close to that of Hopkins, though, crucially, without Hopkins' humorlessness or the simplemindedness and *morbidezza* of his imitative harmony. Perhaps it is simply that in the subsistence economy of Mr. Singer's art, things, denied the luxury of emotion, seem naturally to possess this hardness and effulgence, to become declarative.

This vibrant externality is not, of course, merely applied; it is fundamental to the remarkable concreteness with which the theme common to almost all of Mr. Singer's fiction is rendered: the extraordinary fragility of the cosmic order, the way in which the world is sustained on a pinpoint of grace. It is a fiction replete with false visions and false prophets, lies, dreams, heresies, pretenses, vanities, miracles, devils, imps not born, men called back from death, all these cracks and discontinuities in the cosmic order; replete, that is, with everything that, twisted, meager, fragmentary, incomplete, stands apart from the universe and its will. The *shtetl* tales are of two sorts—demonic stories and moral tales—and both bear on the one theme. The former are terrible and seductive celebrations—Mr. Singer is generally of the devil's party—of the destruction of the cosmic order, in which the prudence, ritual regularity, and meditation on the Law which alone maintain this order are, through the deceits of quite literal demons, swept away by enthusiasm and idolatry. In the moral tales, the Manicheism latent in these demonics is dissolved and the gaps in the cosmic order are shown not to be gaps at all. The moral of Mr. Singer's celebrated "Gimpel the Fool" is of this sort: "I wandered over the land, and good people did not neglect me. After many years I became old and white; I heard a great deal, many lies and falsehoods, but the longer I lived the more I understood that there were really no lies. Whatever doesn't really happen is dreamed at night. It happens to one if it doesn't happen to another, tomorrow if not today, or a century hence if not next year."

Again, in "The Beggar Said So" of this volume, a less-than-lie, mere babble, something perhaps never uttered at all, becomes, years later, a fulfilled prophecy. Or, in "A Piece of Advice," a wonder-working rabbi counsels an Angry Man to cure himself by playing the flatterer, for "[T]he Almighty does not require good intentions. The deed is what counts. It is what you do that matters. Are you angry perhaps? Go ahead and be angry, but speak gentle words and be friendly at the same times. Are you afraid of being a dissembler? So what if you pretend to be something you aren't? For whose sake are you lying? For your Father in Heaven, His Holy Name, blessed be He, knows the intention and the intention behind the intention, and it is this that is the main thing." We may see in this, I think, the deeper issue of Mr. Singer's externalizing style. Intention is merely subjective, merely personal, and only by his behavior, by manifesting himself in cry and gesture, does the person come to take his place in the cosmic order. The values of the *shtetl*-world are entirely communal: just as personal feeling is absorbed by custom, by the congregation, by the background of the Diaspora, by God, so the religious does not reside in what transpires in the soul but in how one appears before the community and congregation; for, like the cosmic order which it articulates, the Law is ex-

ternal. But this—the fusion of the ethical act with the act of faith—
is the very ground of Judaism upon which the *shtetl* itself rests. The
crux of Mr. Singer's stories is often to be found in the period of wavering
"between a yes and a no"; and Hindele's madness is identical with
her refusal to cry out, just as the dreadful sin of Lise, the unrepentant
adultress of "The Destruction of Kreshev," is her final silence. Even
Mr. Singer's conventional plots and settings—handled so lovingly they
are touched with inevitability—seem to possess this gestural quality.
I am thinking particularly of my favorite story in this volume, "In the
Poor-house," where, under the low heaven of the poorhouse ceiling,
several remnant-lives slowly dilate with their life stories and philoso-
phizing, and then subside. And yet it is a question whether the sources
of Mr. Singer's art are so ethical as I have been making out its final
effect to be. It is not simply that he is of the devil's party but that the
very crackling and passion of his style seem to come from his demons,
these smashers of the cosmic order who let loose from the broken ends
of things that formed vitality which is joy. But, perhaps, it is only that
I don't understand Mr. Singer's faith.

Cynthia Ozick

Edelshtein's friendship with Baumzweig had a ferocious secret: it was moored entirely to their agreed hatred for the man they called *der chazer*. He was named Pig because of his extraordinarily white skin, like a tissue of pale ham, and also because in the last decade he had become unbelievably famous. When they did not call him Pig they called him *shed*—Devil. They also called him Yankee Doodle. His name was Yankel Ostrover, and he was a writer of stories.

They hated him for the amazing thing that had happened to him—his fame—but this they never referred to. Instead they discussed his style: his Yiddish was impure, his sentences lacked grace and sweep, his paragraph transitions were amateur, vile. Or else they raged against his subject matter, which was insanely sexual, pornographic, paranoid, freakish—men who embraced men, women who caressed women, sodomists of every variety, boys copulating with hens, butchers who drank blood for strength behind the knife. All the stories were set in an imaginary Polish village, Zwrdl, and by now there was almost no American literary intellectual alive who had not learned to say Zwrdl when he meant lewd. Ostrover's wife was reputed to be a high-born Polish Gentile woman from the "real" Zwrdl, the daughter in fact of a minor princeling, who did not know a word of Yiddish and read her husband's fiction falteringly, in English translation—but both Edelshtein and Baumzweig had encountered her often enough over the years, at this meeting and that, and regarded her as no more impressive than a pot of stale fish. Her Yiddish had an unpleasant gargling Galician accent, her vocabulary was a thin soup—they joked that it was correct to say she spoke no Yiddish—and she mewed it like a peasant, comparing prices. She was a short square woman, a cube with low-slung

From "Envy; or, Yiddish in America," in *The Pagan Rabbi and Other Stories*, by Cynthia Ozick (New York: Alfred A. Knopf, 1971), 46–48, 62–63. Reprinted by permission of Random House, Inc.

udders and a flat backside. It was partly Ostrover's mockery, partly his self-advertising, that had converted her into a little princess. He would make her go into their bedroom to get a whip he claimed she had used on her bay, Romeo, trotting over her father's lands in her girlhood. Baumzweig often said this same whip was applied to the earlobes of Ostrover's translators, unhappy pairs of collaborators he changed from month to month, never satisfied.

Ostrover's glory was exactly in this: that he required translators. Though he wrote only in Yiddish, his fame was American, national, international. They considered him a "modern." Ostrover was free of the prison of Yiddish! Out, out—he had burst out, he was in the world of reality.

And how had he begun? The same as anybody, a columnist for one of the Yiddish dailies, a humorist, a cheap fast article-writer, a squeezer-out of real-life tales. Like anybody else, he saved up a few dollars, put a paper clip over his stories, and hired a Yiddish press to print up a hundred copies. A book. Twenty-five copies he gave to people he counted as relatives, another twenty-five he sent to enemies and rivals, the rest he kept under his bed in the original cartons. Like anybody else, his literary gods were Chekhov and Tolstoy, Peretz and Sholem Aleichem. From this, how did he come to *The New Yorker*, to *Playboy*, to big lecture fees, invitations to Yale and M.I.T. and Vassar, to the Midwest, to Buenos Aires, to a literary agent, to a publisher on Madison Avenue?

"He sleeps with the right translators," Paula said. Edelshtein gave out a whinny. He knew some of Ostrover's translators—a spinster hack in dresses below the knee, occasionally a certain half-mad and drunken lexicographer, college boys with a dictionary.

Q: Mr. Ostrover, what would you say is the symbolic weight of this story?

A: The symbolic weight is, what you need you deserve. If you don't need to be knocked on the head you'll never deserve it.

Q: Sir, I'm writing a paper on you for my English class. Can you tell me please if you believe in hell?

A: Not since I got rich.

Q: How about God? Do you believe in God?

A: Exactly the way I believe in pneumonia. If you have pneumonia, you have it. If you don't, you don't.

Q: Is it true your wife is a Countess? Some people say she's really only Jewish.

A: In religion she's a transvestite, and in actuality she's a Count.

Q: Is there really such a language as Zwrdlish?

A: You're speaking it right now, it's the language of fools.

Q: What would happen if you weren't translated into English?

A: The pygmies and the Eskimos would read me instead. Nowadays to be Ostrover is to be a worldwide industry.

Q: Then why don't you write about worldwide things like wars?

A: Because I'm afraid of loud noises.

Q: What do you think of the future of Yiddish?

A: What do you think of the future of the Doberman pinscher?

Q: People say other Yiddishists envy you.

A: No, it's I who envy them. I like a quiet life.

Q: Do you keep the Sabbath?

A: Of course, didn't you notice it's gone?—I keep it hidden.

Q: And the dietary laws? Do you observe them?

A: Because of the moral situation of the world I have to. I was heartbroken to learn that the minute an oyster enters my stomach, he becomes an anti-Semite. A bowl of shrimp once started a pogrom against my intestines.

Jokes, jokes! It looked to go on for another hour. The condition of fame, a Question Period: a man can stand up forever and dribble shallow quips and everyone admires him for it.

Jacob Glatstein

If we examine more closely the fortuitous growth of Bashevis' fame, we find that Bashevis enjoys today a much more important place in American literature, where he has more friends and is read with greater interest, than in Yiddish literature. The Yiddish reader is much less enthusiastic over Bashevis Singer's unpleasant stories than his non-Jewish reader, who enjoys his work tremendously. The Yiddish reader, for the most part, derives pleasure from the enjoyment that Bashevis gives the outside world, but is personally less enthusiastic over Bashevis' tales of horror and eroticism.

It is therefore really puzzling why a writer so deeply rooted in the Yiddish language should find greater acceptance in the stranger's world than in his own. Perhaps there is an answer, but this particular answer makes it even more puzzling. A Bashevis story has a Jewish facade, but paradoxically it reads better and pleasanter in English than in the original Yiddish. His stories are more attuned to the non-Jewish than to the Jewish reader, to whom Bashevis' themes are a distasteful blend of superstition and shoddy mysticism. Jews have warmly accepted the kind of mystic literature that exuded exaltation and sanctity; but non-Jewish readers have long been thrilled by supernatural mysteries, spine-chillers and horror tales.

Bashevis became famous primarily because of his short stories. His longer narratives such as *The Magician of Lublin* and *The Slave* have for the most part been carried along by the impetus of his fame as a teller of tales of horror and lust. When Bashevis published his *Family Moskat* in English, the novel was sharply criticized. Recently, he refurbished it and expected it to receive a warm welcome, but the response was very meagre. Isaac Bashevis Singer's reputation is anchored mainly on his short stories.

Abraham Reisin once told me that he never "killed" one of his heroes. It seems to me that this Jewish trait of humaneness has char-

From "The Fame of Bashevis Singer," *Congress Bi-Weekly*, 27 December 1969, pp. 17–19. Reprinted by permission of the American Jewish Congress.

acterized Yiddish literature; and even if not all writers were as compassionate as Reisin, Yiddish literature did not commit any wild and perverse crimes against its heroes. With rare exceptions, they were allowed to live out their allotted years and they certainly were never consciously dragged through all kinds of spiritual and physical depravity.

Bashevis is possibly the first Yiddish writer to put his so-called heroes on the same level with the heroes in non-Jewish literature. He dehumanized them, forcing them to commit the most ugly deeds. He brutalized them and made them so obnoxious that the Yiddish reader was repelled by them. The non-Jewish reader, however, has long been accustomed to such treatment of literary heroes. Further, for the Yiddish reader Bashevis' superstitious stories savor of a warmed-over stew of hoary old wives' tales, made alien by villainy, brutality and cynicism. Jews have never dealt with such literature and only Bashevis introduced this nether-world into his Jewish stories.

Glossary

Chanukah: holiday celebrating rededication of the Temple in Jerusalem in 165 B.C.E.

Diaspora: from the Greek for "dispersion," that is, the Jews living outside the Holy Land

dybbuk: a condemned spirit who inhabits the body of a living person and controls his or her actions

ein-sof: literally, "without end"; a cabalistic term for that aspect of the godhead about which nothing can be thought or said

Eretz Israel: the Land of Israel

galut: exile; condition of Jewish people in exile

Gemarah: section of the Talmud interpreting the Mishnah

goy: a gentile, a non-Jew; literally, Hebrew for "nation"

halakhah: that part of Jewish literature which deals with religious, ethical, civil, and criminal law

Hasidim: religious enthusiasts, devotees of hasidism, or "pietism," a religious revival beginning in the eighteenth century

kaddish: literally "sanctification," but usually refers to memorial prayer for the dead

lamed-vov: Hebrew for the number 36; according to a statement in the Talmud (Sanhedrin 97b), "the world must contain not less than 36 righteous men vouchsafed the sight of the Divine Presence"

Mishnah: earliest codification of the oral Law, which is the basis of the Talmud

Passover: festival of unleavened bread, commemorating the exodus of the children of Israel from Egypt

Purim: holiday commemorating the deliverance of the Jews of Persia from destruction, as told in the biblical book of Esther

rebbetsin: wife of a rabbi or teacher

schlemiel: a foolish and powerless but sometimes also wise and saintly individual

129

sefirot: literally "numbers" in Hebrew, plural form of *sefira*; cabalistic term for emanations and manifestations of the godhead

Shechinah: divine presence

Shevuot: Feast of the Pentecost; festival commemorating the giving of the Torah to Moses

shtetl: Jewish town or village of Eastern Europe

Shulchan Aruch: "Prepared Table," standard code of Jewish law compiled by Joseph Karo and first published in 1565

Simchat Torah: "Rejoicing of the Law," a holiday celebration

Talmud: result and record of eight centuries of study and discussion of the Bible by Jewish scholars in the academies of Palestine and Babylonia

Torah: narrowly, the Pentateuch, but by extension all Jewish teaching

yeshiva: institute for higher learning in Judaism

Yom Kippur: Day of Atonement

Chronology

1904   Isaac Singer born 14 July in Radzymin, Poland. (The name Bashevis—derived from his mother's name, Bathsheva—was later added in signing published works, which in Yiddish bear only the name Isaac Bashevis.)

1908   Singer family moves to Warsaw.

1914   Begins to read non-Jewish writers, especially Dostoyevski, and to experience religious doubt.

1917   Moves, with mother, to Bilgoray for four years.

1918–1920   Begins to write poems and stories in Hebrew and becomes a Hebrew teacher in a "worldly" school for boys and girls of Bilgoray. Falls under the influence of Spinoza.

1921   Enrolls at Tachkemoni Rabbinical Seminary in Warsaw but remains only a year before returning to Bilgoray.

1923   Becomes a proofreader for *Literarishe Bletter*, a Yiddish literary magazine in Warsaw. Begins translating modern fiction (Hamsun, Zweig, Thomas Mann) into Yiddish.

1925   Publishes first story, "In Old Age," in *Literarishe Bletter*.

1926–1927   Publishes "Grandchildren" and "A Village Gravedigger" in *Warshawer Shriften*.

1929   A son, Israel, born to Singer and his Communist mistress, Runia.

1933   Writes first novel, *Satan in Goray*, published serially in *Globus* (a Yiddish journal coedited by Singer) and in book form in 1935.

1935   Moves to the United States, taking up life in Williamsburgh section of Brooklyn. Begins to write for *Jewish Daily Forward*.

1935–1936   *The Sinning Messiah: A Historical Novel* serialized in *Forward*.

1940 Marries Alma Haimann.

1943 Publishes four new stories ("The Destruction of Kreshev," "Diary of One Not Born," "Zeidlus the Pope," and "Two Corpses Go Dancing") in Yiddish reissue of *Satan in Goray.*

1944 Israel Joshua Singer, his novelist older brother, dies.

1945 Begins work on *The Family Moskat*, published serially in the *Forward*, 1945–1948.

1950 Publishes *The Family Moskat* in book form, both in Yiddish and in English, his first novel to appear in English translation.

1953 Short story "Gimpel the Fool," translated by Saul Bellow, appears in *Partisan Review* and introduces Singer to non-Jewish audiences.

1955 *Satan in Goray* appears in English translation by Jacob Sloan.

1957 *Shadows on the Hudson* serialized in the *Forward.* Publication of first collection of short stories in translation, *Gimpel the Fool and Other Stories.*

1958 *A Ship to America* published serially in *Forward.*

1959 *The Magician of Lublin* serialized in *Forward.*

1960 *The Magican of Lublin* published in English translation.

1961 *The Spinoza of Market Street and Other Stories.*

1962 *The Slave.*

1964 *Short Friday and Other Stories.* Elected to National Institute of Arts and Letters.

1966 *In My Father's Court* (autobiographical memoir).

1967 *The Manor* (written between 1953 and 1955).

1968 *The Séance and Other Stories. When Shlemiel Went to Warsaw* (children's book).

1969 *The Estate.*

1970 *A Day of Pleasure* wins National Book Award for Children's Books. *A Friend of Kafka and Other Stories.*

1972 *Enemies, a Love Story.*

1973 *A Crown of Feathers and Other Stories.*

1974 National Book Award. *The Penitent* (in Yiddish).

1975 *Passions and Other Stories.*

1976 *Yarme and Kayle* (in Yiddish).

1978 *A Young Man in Search of Love. Shosha.* Receives Nobel Prize in literature.

1979 *Old Love and Other Stories.*

1980 Visits U.S. Military Academy at West Point, reviews troops, gives lecture.

1981 *Lost in America.*

1982 *The Collected Stories.*

1983 *The Penitent.*

1985 *The Image and Other Stories.*

1988 *The Death of Methuselah and Other Stories. The King of the Fields.*

Selected Bibliography

Primary Works

Short Story Collections

The Collected Stories of Isaac Bashevis Singer. New York: Farrar, Straus & Giroux, 1982. ("Gimpel the Fool," "The Gentleman from Cracow," "Joy," "The Little Shoemakers," "The Unseen," "The Spinoza of Market Street," "The Destruction of Kreshev," "Taibele and Her Demon," "Alone," "Yentl the Yeshiva Boy," "Zeidlus the Pope," "The Last Demon," "Short Friday," "The Séance," "The Slaughterer," "The Dead Fiddler," "Henne Fire," "The Letter Writer," "A Friend of Kafka," "The Cafeteria," "The Joke," "Powers," "Something Is There," "A Crown of Feathers," "A Day in Coney Island," "The Cabalist of East Broadway," "A Quotation from Klopstock," "A Dance and a Hop," "Grandfather and Grandson," "Old Love," "The Admirer," "The Yearning Heifer," "A Tale of Two Sisters," "Three Encounters," "Passions," "Brother Beetle," "The Betrayer of Israel," "The Psychic Journey," "The Manuscript," "The Power of Darkness," "The Bus," "A Night in the Poorhouse," "Escape from Civilization," "Vanvild Kava," "The Reencounter," "Neighbors," "Moon and Madness.")

A Crown of Feathers and Other Stories. New York: Farrar, Straus & Giroux, 1973. ("A Crown of Feathers," "A Day in Coney Island," "The Captive," "The Blizzard," "Property," "The Lantuch," "The Son from America," "The Briefcase," "The Cabalist of East Broadway," "The Bishop's Robe," "A Quotation from Klopstock," "The Magazine," "Lost," "The Prodigy," "The Third One," "The Recluse," "A Dance and a Hop," "Her Son," "The Egotist," "The Beard," "The Dance," "On a Wagon," "Neighbors," "Grandfather and Grandson.")

The Death of Methuselah and Other Stories. New York: Farrar, Straus & Giroux, 1988. ("The Jew from Babylon," "The House Friend," "Burial at Sea," "The Recluse," "Disguised," "The Accuser and the Accused," "The Trap," "The Smuggler," "A Peephole in the Gate," "The Bitter Truth," "The Impresario," "Logarithms," "Gifts," "Runners to Nowhere," "The Missing Line," "The Hotel," "Dazzled," "Sabbath in Gehenna," "The Last Gaze," "The Death of Methuselah.")

A Friend of Kafka and Other Stories. New York: Farrar, Straus & Giroux, 1970.

("A Friend of Kafka," "Guests on a Winter Night," "The Key," "Dr. Beeber," "Stories from behind the Stove," "The Cafeteria," "The Mentor," "Pigeons," "The Chimney Sweep," "The Riddle," "Altele," "The Joke," "The Primper," "Schloimele," "The Colony," "The Blasphemer," "The Wager," "The Son," "Fate," "Powers," "Something Is There.")

Gimpel the Fool and Other Stories. New York: Noonday Press, 1957. ("Gimpel the Fool," "The Gentleman from Cracow," "The Wife Killer," "By the Light of Memorial Candles," "The Mirror," "The Little Shoemakers," "Joy," "From the Diary of One Not Born," "The Old Man," "Fire," "The Unseen.")

The Image and Other Stories. New York: Farrar, Straus & Giroux, 1985. ("Advice," "One Day of Happiness," "The Bond," "The Interview," "The Divorce," "Strong as Death Is Love," "Why Heisherik Was Born," "The Enemy," "Remnants," "On the Way to the Poorhouse," "Loshikl," "The Pocket Remembered," "The Secret," "A Nest Egg for Paradise," "The Conference," "Miracles," "The Litigants," "A Telephone Call on Yom Kippur," "Strangers," "The Mistake," "Confused," "The Image.")

Old Love and Other Stories. New York: Farrar, Straus & Giroux, 1979. ("One Night in Brazil," "Yochna and Shmelke," "Two," "The Psychic Journey," "Elka and Meir," "A Party in Miami Beach," "Two Weddings and One Divorce," "A Cage for Satan," "Brother Beetle," "The Boy Knows the Truth," "There Are No Coincidences," "Not for the Sabbath," "The Safe Deposit," "The Betrayer of Israel," "Tanhum," "Contents," "The Manuscript," "The Power of Darkness," "The Bus.")

Passions and Other Stories. New York: Farrar, Straus & Giroux, 1975. ("Hanka," "Old Love," "Errors," "The Admirer," "Sabbath in Portugal," "The Yearning Heifer," "The Witch," "Sam Palka and David Vishkover," "A Tutor in the Village," "The New Year Party," "A Tale of Two Sisters," "A Pair," "The Fatalist," "Two Markets," "The Gravedigger," "The Sorcerer," "Moishele," "Three Encounters," "The Adventure," "Passions.")

The Séance and Other Stories. New York: Farrar, Straus & Giroux, 1968. ("The Séance," "The Slaughterer," "The Dead Fiddler," "The Lecture," "Cockadoodledoo," "The Plagiarist," "Zeitl and Rickel," "The Warehouse," "Henne Fire," "Getzel the Monkey," "Yanda," "The Needle," "Two Corpses Go Dancing," "The Parrot," "The Brooch," "The Letter Writer.")

Short Friday and Other Stories. New York: Farrar, Straus & Giroux, 1964. ("Taibele and Her Demon," "Big and Little," "Blood," "Alone," "Esther Kreindel the Second," "Jachid and Jechidah," "Under the Knife," "The Fast," "The Last Demon," "Yentl the Yeshiva Boy," "Three Tales,"

Selected Bibliography

"Zeidlus the Pope," "A Wedding in Brownsville," "I Place My Reliance on No Man," "Cunegunde," "Short Friday.")

The Spinoza of Market Street and Other Stories. New York: Farrar, Straus & Giroux, 1961. ("The Spinoza of Market Street," "The Black Wedding," "A Tale of Two Liars," "The Shadow of a Crib," "Shiddah and Kuziba," "Caricature," "The Beggar Said So," "The Man Who Came Back," "A Piece of Advice," "In the Poorhouse," "The Destruction of Kreshev.")

Uncollected Short Stories

"The Boudoir." *Vogue*, 1 April 1966, 148–49, 214.

"Converts." *Commentary* 38 (December 1964): 46–48.

"Dalfunka Where the Rich Live Forever." *New York Times Magazine*, 28 March 1976, 111.

"Hail, the Messiah." In *Jewish Stories of Today*, ed. Morris Kreitman. London: Faber & Faber, 1958.

"A Hanukkah Story." *Good Housekeeping*, December 1982, 94.

"My Adventures as an Idealist." *Saturday Evening Post*, 18 November 1967, 68–73.

"Ole and Trufa: A Story of Two Leaves." *Atlantic Monthly*, January 1979, 40–41.

"One Day of Happiness." *Cavalier*, September 1965, 19, 78–84.

"The Prodigal Fool." *Saturday Evening Post*, 26 February 1966, 64–66, 68–69.

"Sacrifice." *Harper's*, February 1964, 61–64.

"The Strong." *American Judaism* 15 (Winter 1965–66): 20–21.

"Twice Chanukah." *Ladies' Home Journal*, December 1985, 72.

Novels in English

Enemies, a Love Story. New York: Farrar, Straus & Giroux, 1972. Published serially in Yiddish in the *Forward* in 1966.

The Estate. New York: Farrar, Straus & Giroux, 1969. A continuation of the work first published serially in Yiddish in the *Forward* from 1953 to 1955.

The Family Moskat. New York: Noonday Press, 1950. Published in Yiddish serially in *Forward* from 1945 to 1948 and in book form 1950.

The King of the Fields. New York: Farrar, Straus & Giroux, 1988.

The Magician of Lublin. New York: Noonday Press, 1960. Published serially in Yiddish in the *Forward* in 1959.

The Manor. New York: Farrar, Straus & Giroux, 1967. Published serially in Yiddish in the *Forward* from 1953 to 1955. A one-volume edition of *The Manor* and its continuation, *The Estate*, was published by Farrar, Straus in 1979.

The Penitent. New York: Farrar, Straus & Giroux, 1983. Published serially in Yiddish in the *Forward* in 1974.

Satan in Goray. New York: Noonday Press, 1955. Originally published in Yiddish in 1934–1935.

Shosha. New York: Farrar, Straus & Giroux, 1978. Published serially in Yiddish in the *Forward* in 1974.

The Slave. New York: Farrar, Straus & Giroux, 1962. Published serially in Yiddish in the *Forward* in 1961.

Novels in Yiddish

Shadows on the Hudson. Serialized in the *Forward* in 1957.
A Ship to America. Serialized in the *Forward* in 1958.
The Sinning Messiah. Serialized in the *Forward* in 1935–1936.
Yarme and Kayle. Serialized in the *Forward* in 1976.

Memoirs

In My Father's Court. New York: Farrar, Straus & Giroux, 1966.
A Little Boy in Search of God; or, Mysticism in a Personal Light. Garden City, N.Y.: Doubleday, 1976.
Lost in America. Garden City, N.Y.: Doubleday, 1981.
Love and Exile. Garden City, N.Y.: Doubleday, 1984. Combines *A Little Boy in Search of God, A Young Man in Search of Love,* and *Lost in America.*
A Young Man in Search of Love. Garden City, N.Y.: Doubleday, 1978.

Children's Books

Alone in the Wild Forest. New York: Farrar, Straus & Giroux, 1971.
A Day of Pleasure. New York: Farrar, Straus & Giroux, 1970.
Elijah the Slave. New York: Farrar, Straus & Giroux, 1970.
The Fearsome Inn. New York: Scribner's, 1967.
The Fools of Chelm and Their History. New York: Farrar, Straus & Giroux, 1973.
The Golem. New York: Farrar, Straus & Giroux, 1982.
Joseph and Koza; or, The Sacrifice to the Vistula. New York: Farrar, Straus & Giroux, 1970.
Mazel and Shlimazel; or, The Milk of a Lioness. New York: Farrar, Straus & Giroux, 1967.
Naftali the Storyteller and His Horse, Sus, and Other Stories. New York: Farrar, Straus & Giroux, 1976.
The Power of Light: Eight Stories for Hanukkah. New York: Farrar, Straus & Giroux, 1980.
Stories for Children. New York: Farrar, Straus & Giroux, 1984.
A Tale of Three Wishes. New York: Farrar, Straus & Giroux, 1975.
The Topsy-Turvy Emperor of China. New York: Harper & Row, 1971.
When Shlemiel Went to Warsaw and Other Stories. New York: Farrar, Straus & Giroux, 1968.

Selected Bibliography

Why Noah Chose the Dove. New York: Farrar, Straus & Giroux, 1974.
The Wicked City. New York: Farrar, Straus & Giroux, 1972.
Zlateh the Goat and Other Stories. New York: Harper & Row, 1966.

Nonfiction

"The Extreme Jews." *Harper's*, April 1967, 55–62.
"Freedom and Literature." *Parameters* 9 (1981): 8–12.
"The Future of Yiddish and Yiddish Literature." *Jewish Book Annual* 25 (1967): 70–74.
"Indecent Language and Sex in Literature." *Jewish Heritage* 8 (Summer 1965): 51–54.
Introduction to *Hunger*, by Knut Hamsun. New York: Noonday Press, 1968.
Introduction to *Yoshe Kalb*, by I. J. Singer. New York: Harper and Row, 1965.
"Kafka's Trials." *Book Week*, 1 May 1966, 16–17.
"A New Use for Yiddish." *Commentary* 33 (March 1962): 267–69.
Nobel Lecture. New York: Farrar, Straus & Giroux, 1979. Also includes "Why I Write for Children," Singer's statement prepared for the occasion of his acceptance of the National Book Award for Children's Books in 1970.
"Once on Second Avenue There Lived a Yiddish Theater." *New York Times*, 17 April 1966, sec. 2, p. 3.
"The Poetry of Faith." *Commentary* 32 (September 1961): 258–60.
"Problems of Yiddish Prose in America." *Prooftexts* 9 (January 1989): 5–12.
"Roth and Singer on Bruno Schulz." *New York Times Book Review*, 13 February 1977, 5, 14, 16, 20.
"Sholom Aleichem: Spokesman for a People." *New York Times*, 20 September 1964, sec. 2, pp. 1, 4.
"What's in It for Me?" *Harper's*, October 1965, 166–67.

Secondary Works

Interviews

Andersen, David M. "Isaac Bashevis Singer: Conversations in California." *Modern Fiction Studies* 16 (Winter 1970–71): 424–39.
Blocker, Joel, and Richard Elman. "An Interview with Isaac Bashevis Singer." *Commentary* 36 (November 1963): 364–72.
Burgin, Richard, and Isaac Bashevis Singer. *Conversations with Isaac Bashevis Singer.* New York: Doubleday, 1985.
Gilman, Sander L. "Interview/Isaac Bashevis Singer." *Diacritics* 4 (Spring 1974): 30–33.
Lee, Grace Farrell. "Stewed Prunes and Rice Pudding: College Students Eat

Selected Bibliography

and Talk with Isaac Bashevis Singer." *Contemporary Literature* 19 (Autumn 1978): 446–58.

Pinsker, Sanford. "Isaac Bashevis Singer: An Interview." *Critique* 11 (1969): 26–39.

Ribalow, Reena Sara. "A Visit to Isaac Bashevis Singer." *The Reconstructionist* 30 (29 May 1964): 19–26.

Rosenblatt, Paul, and Gene Koppel. *Isaac Bashevis Singer on Literature and Life.* Tucson: University of Arizona Press, 1971.

Books

Alexander, Edward. *Isaac Bashevis Singer.* Boston: Twayne Publishers, 1980.

Buchen, Irving. *Isaac Bashevis Singer and the Eternal Past.* New York: New York University Press, 1968.

Friedman, Lawrence S. *Understanding Isaac Bashevis Singer.* Columbia: University of South Carolina Press, 1988.

Kresh, Paul. Isaac Bashevis Singer. New York: Dial Press, 1979.

Lee, Grace Farrell. *From Exile to Redemption: The Fiction of Isaac Bashevis Singer.* Carbondale and Edwardsville: Southern Illinois University Press, 1987.

Irving Malin, ed. *Critical Views of Isaac Bashevis Singer.* New York: New York University Press, 1969.

———. *Isaac Bashevis Singer.* New York: Ungar, 1972.

Milbauer, Asher Zelig. *Transcending Exile: Conrad, Nabokov, I. B. Singer.* Miami: Florida International University Press, 1985.

Miller, David N. *Fear of Fiction: Narrative Strategies in the Works of Isaac Bashevis Singer.* Albany: State University of New York Press, 1985.

———, ed. *Recovering the Canon.* Leiden: E. J. Brill, 1986.

Siegel, Ben. *Isaac Bashevis Singer.* Minneapolis: University of Minnesota Press, 1969.

Articles and Parts of Books

Alexander, Edward. "The Destruction and Resurrection of the Jews in the Fiction of Isaac Bashevis Singer." In *The Resonance of Dust: Essays on Holocaust Literature and Jewish Fate.* Columbus: Ohio State University Press, 1979.

———. "Isaac Bashevis Singer and Jewish Utopianism." In *The Jewish Idea and Its Enemies.* New Brunswick and Oxford: Transaction Books, 1988.

Baumgarten, Murray. "Clothing and Character." In *City Scriptures: Modern Jewish Writing.* Cambridge, Mass.: Harvard University Press, 1982.

Berger, Alan L. "Isaac Bashevis Singer." In *Crisis and Covenant: The Holocaust in American Jewish Fiction*, 79–88. Albany: State University of New York Press, 1985.

Feldman, Irving. "The Shtetl World." *Kenyon Review* 24 (Winter 1962): 173–77.

Selected Bibliography

Fixler, Michael. "The Redeemers: Themes in the Fiction of Isaac Bashevis Singer." *Kenyon Review* 26 (Spring 1964): 371–86.

Glatstein, Jacob. "The Fame of Bashevis Singer." *Congress Bi-Weekly* 32 (27 December 1965): 17–19.

Howe, Irving. Introduction to *Selected Short Stories of Isaac Bashevis Singer*. New York: Modern Library, 1966.

———, and I. B. Singer. "Yiddish Tradition vs. Jewish Tradition: A Dialogue." *Midstream* 19 (June/July 1973): 33–38.

Pinsker, Sanford. "The Fictive Worlds of Isaac Bashevis Singer." *Critique* 11 (1969): 26–39.

P[rager], L[eonard]. "Isaac Bashevis Singer." *Encyclopedia Judaica*, vol. 4, B. Jerusalem: Keter, 1971.

Reichek, Morton A. "Storyteller." *New York Times Magazine*, 23 March 1975, 16–18, 20, 22, 24, 26, 28, 30, 33.

Shmeruk, Chone. "Bashevis Singer—In Search of His Autobiography." *Jewish Quarterly* 29 (Winter 1981–82): 28–36.

Zatlin, Linda G. "The Themes of Isaac Bashevis Singer's Short Fiction." *Critique* 11 (1969): 40–46.

Bibliographies

Bryer, Jackson R., and Paul E. Rockwell. "Isaac Bashevis Singer in English: A Bibliography." In *Critical Views of Isaac Bashevis Singer*, ed. Irving Malin. New York: New York University Press, 1968.

Miller, David Neal. *Bibliography of Isaac Bashevis Singer: 1924–1949*. New York, Berne, Frankfort on the Main: Peter Lang, 1983.

———. *A Bibliography of Isaac Bashevis Singer, January 1950–June 1952*. Working Papers in Yiddish and East European Jewish Culture, vol. 34. New York: YIVO Institute for Jewish Research, 1979.

Index

Abraham and Isaac. *See* Biblical references
America, 10–11, 32, 74; in Singer's fiction, 92; Singer and, 92; *See also* American Jewry
American Jewish life, 10–11, 34, 74
American Jewry, 30, 33–34, 74; Singer on, 10–11, 92
American Judaism, 75
American literature and Singer, 50, 126
American readership and Singer, 10–11, 107, 114
anarchism, 41–42
An-Ski, S.: *The Dybbuk*, 115
Apocalypse, tales of, 3, 35–42
Apocalyptic temper, 38, 108; in Eastern European Jewry, 112
Aramaic, 91
archetypes, 3, 29, 31, 33–34
Arendt, Hannah, 53
Aristotle, 98
Asch, Sholem, 81, 84
assimilation: as a faith, 47; in Singer's fiction, 12–13, 33–34; Singer on, 91, 93; *See also* American Jewry
atheism, 15, 16, 44, 47, 48; *See also* disbelief, materialism, naturalism
atheists, 56–57

Balfour Declaration, 115
Bellow, Saul, 50
Bible, 12, 35, 44, 47, 94; and Jewish history, 32, 44; and modern Jewish history, 31–34; and symbolism, 93; Book of Ezekiel, 35; Singer on the, 88, 97, 120
Biblical references: Abraham and Isaac, 29, 31, 33, 46, 110; Jacob and Esau, 33, 47
Bilgoray. *See* Poland
Bolsheviks, 10, 116
Buddhism, 42, 95

Cabalism, 16, 35, 39, 61, 112
Carlyle, Thomas, 19, 42, 44
characters. *See* fictional characters
Chasidism. *See* Hasidism
Chaucer, Geoffrey, 3
Chekhov, Anton, 97, 98
children, role of, in Singer's fiction, 37, 38, 44, 47, 49, 57, 60, 107
Chmielnicki, Bogdan, pogroms of, 31, 33, 35, 110, 112
Christianity, 23, 46, 48–49, 56, 62
collective vs. personal Jewish fate in Singer's fiction, 110
Communism, 10; Singer on, 85
Communists, Jewish, 41
cruelty and God, 90–91

death, 33; and burial, 48; life as, 14–15
democracy, Singer on, 85
demonic, 18, 121; Singer on the, 85–86
demonism in Sabbateanism, 112
demons. *See* devils
details, importance of, in Singer's fiction, 117
detachment in Singer's fiction, 116–17
devils and demons, 11–12, 14, 16–19 *passim*, 38, 44, 48, 51, 57–58, 60, 106, 108, 111, 114, 121, 122; as false redeemers, 36–38; *See also* supernatural

The Author

Edward Alexander received his B.A. from Columbia University and his M.A. (1959) and Ph.D. (1963) from the University of Minnesota. He is currently professor of English at the University of Washington in Seattle. He has also taught at Tufts University, Tel-Aviv University, Hebrew University, and Memphis State University, where he held the Bornblum Chair of Excellence in Judaic Studies in 1988.

His books on Victorian literature include *Matthew Arnold and John Stuart Mill, John Morley*, and *Arnold, Ruskin, and the Modern Temper*. He is also the editor of *John Stuart Mill: Literary Essays*.

His books on Jewish subjects are *The Resonance of Dust, Isaac Bashevis Singer*, and *The Jewish Idea and Its Enemies*.

He has published essays in the *University of Toronto Quarterly, Modern Language Review, Journal of English and Germanic Philology, Dickensian, Midstream, Encounter, American Spectator, Commentary, Judaism, Congress Monthly*, and numerous other journals. His awards include Fulbright, American Council of Learned Societies, Guggenheim, and National Foundation for Jewish Culture fellowships.

The Editor

Gordon Weaver earned his Ph.D. in English and creative writing at the University of Denver, and is currently professor of English at Oklahoma State University. He is the author of several novels, including *Count a Lonely Cadence, Give Him a Stone, Circling Byzantium,* and most recently *The Eight Corners of the World.* His short stories are collected in *The Entombed Man of Thule, Such Waltzing Was Not Easy, Getting Serious, Morality Play,* and *A World Quite Round.* Recognition of his fiction includes the St. Lawrence Award for Fiction (1973), two National Endowment for the Arts fellowships (1974 and 1989), and the O. Henry First Prize (1979). He edited *The American Short Story, 1945–1980: A Critical History* and is currently editor of the *Cimarron Review.* Married and the father of three daughters, he lives in Stillwater, Oklahoma.